Advanced Quality Planning

A Commonsense Guide to AQP and APQP

D.H. Stamatis

Advanced Quality Planning

A Commonsense Guide to AQP and APQP

Productivity Press

Productivity Press
444 Park Avenue South, Suite 604
New York, NY 10016
Telephone:212-686-5900
Fax:212-686-5411
E-mail:info@productivitypress.com

Printed in the United States of America

ISBN 1-53627-258-X

05 04 03 02 01   5 4 3 2 1

To Tim and Stephen

Contents

Figures

Tables

Acknowledgments

I thank Mr. R. Munro for his valuable advice and recommendations in the early stages of this project, Mr. G. Tomlinson for his thoughtful review and suggestions of earlier drafts, Dr. R. Roy for his emotional support and encouragement throughout this project, Mr. W. Winchell for his thorough review of and comments on earlier drafts, and the editors and reviewers of the book for their support and helpful suggestions to make this book a better product.

I thank my clients, who helped me articulate some of the concepts and concerns about advanced quality planning (AQP, or APQP in the automotive sector). Because of them, I learned the reality of APQP. Special thanks are reserved for the Ford Motor Company—the ACD (now Visteon) and the Vehicle Operations divisions—for allowing me the opportunity to do their training. In the process, I have learned to appreciate their focus and methodology, and to understand why APQP is an indispensable tool in the quality process. I also thank Mr. W. McCarthy for his valuable contribution to the entire project and especially for the business plan.

Finally, I acknowledge all my seminar participants—over the years—for their suggestions and insights into the APQP process. I have learned a lot from them and hope that, in writing about APQP, I have done justice to their suggestions.

Preface

Once undisputed leaders in the world, American companies' command of markets has eroded. To be sure, though macro-economic factors like the exchange rate and trade policies have harmed our ability to compete, the competitive problems were chiefly the result of ineffective management practices. Among these problems, the lack of planning is the predominant factor in losing the quality edge to foreign markets.

American companies are fighting back. They are addressing all sorts of ways to improve products, services, and return on investment. Some of the more specific items include:

- More focus on quality and customer satisfaction
- Increased numbers of people involved in quality improvement
- Greater teamwork
- Greater positive coverage in newspapers and magazines
- Introduction of international standards (ISO 9000)
- Industry-specific standards (QS-9000, AS9000)
- The Malcolm Baldrige National Quality Award
- Intensified training and education
- Use of statistical methods for quality improvement
- Planning for quality

The results from these changes have been well documented over the past several years. However, these changes have been somewhat disjointed and the competitive position of many of our organizations has not improved substantially. There is now a much greater awareness of the urgency for fundamental change in the way that organizations operate, as well as a recognition that prevention is better than appraisal systems. One realization made by many organizations is the value of the systems approach to planning, specifically as follows:

The necessary fundamental change is that quality must be adopted as a business strategy. This strategy is applicable to all types of organizations including manufacturing and service companies, schools, hospitals, and government agencies. The aim of this strategy is to enable the organization to produce products and services that will be in demand, and to provide a place where people can enjoy their work and take pride in its outcomes.

Quality planning, then becomes the means to accomplish the goals and objectives of the organization, such as increased profits or share of the market, growth, better educated citizens, a cleaner environment, lower costs, higher productivity, or increased return on investment. Deming (1986, p. 3) refers to this as the quality chain reaction. Traditionally, increased quality has been thought to come only at the expense of lower productivity and higher cost. This misconception is a result, in part, of trying to improve quality by inspection or solving problems, rather than by improving products and processes.

If quality is to become a business strategy, top organizational managers must understand quality as a planning strategy and provide leadership for carrying out this strategy. Some important attributes of the planning strategy include:

- Providing methods to reach the goals of the organization
- Sustainable over the long-term
- Balancing internal and external focus

- Compatiblity among different businesses in the organization
- Remaining useful despite changes in the marketplace
- Understandable to and supported by all members of the organization

It has been said many times and in many ways that the difference between planning and not planning may be demonstrated by the "bottom line" of an organization. The difference, of course, is in the attitude and perseverance of the involved individuals. It is a matter of a winning and successful attitude in everything we do. From an advanced quality planning perspective, the "right" attitude may be articulated as illustrated below.

A Winner	A Loser
says, *Let's find out*	says, *Nobody knows*
says, *I was wrong,* when makes a mistake	says, *It wasn't my fault,* when makes a mistake
goes through a problem	*goes around it, and never gets past it*
makes commitments	*makes promises*
listens	*waits until it is their turn to talk*
explains	*defends or explains away*
says, *There should be a better way to do it*	says, *That is the way it's always been done*
paces themself	*has only two speeds— hysterical and lethargic*
focuses on advanced planning	*focuses on appraisals*

The purpose of this book is to set quality planning in the framework of a strategy, using three basic elements:

1. The foundation of the strategy
2. The organization as a system
3. The methods to insure that changes result in the improvement of quality

This book is recommended reading for anyone interested in quality planning.

AUTOMOTIVE APQP

Quality planning is fundamental to the competitiveness of the automotive industry. Applied appropriately, it enhances suppliers' ability to develop and produce products and systems that satisfy their customers. Quality planning in the automotive industry is based on the principles and requirements outlined in the *Advanced Product Quality Planning and Control Plan Reference Manual,* as appropriate to the product or system being supplied to the customer.

Some of the key ingredients of automotive APQP are the following:

SPECIAL CHARACTERISTICS. Cross-functional teams, including the customer where required, identify and agree to product and/or system characteristics during the preparation of FMEAs and Control Plans. Process controls are established for all special characteristics.

FEASIBILITY REVIEWS. Manufacturing feasibility of proposed products and/or systems prior to contracting to produce those products and/or systems. Feasibility studies are documented appropriately.

FAILURE MODE AND EFFECTS ANALYSIS. (Design and Process FMEAs). Efforts to incorporate FMEAs in both design and manufacturing processes to achieve defect prevention rather than defect detection is of major interest. Customer required FMEA approval requirements are met prior to production part approval, as required by the customer. Process FMEAs consider all special characteristics.

CONTROL PLANS. Control plans at the system, subsystem, component, and/or material level, as appropriate, for the products supplied to our customers are required as part of the process control. Control plans are approved by the appropriate customer engineering and/or quality activity unless this approval requirement is waived by the customer. The control plans cover three distinct phases, as appropriate.

- Prototype
- Prelaunch
- Production

In addition, control plans are reviewed and updated as appropriate when any of the following occur:

- The product has changed
- The processes are changed
- The processes become unstable
- The processes become noncapable

ONE

Introduction and Backgound

The foundation of the planning strategy is the improvement of quality. The following methods are but a few ways of approaching the quality improvement process:

- Design a new product
- Redesign an existing product
- Design a new process (including service)
- Redesign an existing process
- Improve the system as a whole

It is usually quite easy for people to list the products they make or services they deliver and to describe the processes that produce them. It is much more difficult, however, to know how to improve the quality of the products or services. Should a new product be designed or should the process that produces the product be redesigned? Should some improvement be made to the system as a whole? The five activities listed above may be carried out within various parts of the organization. These efforts must be coordinated and must focus on a common purpose. The foundation of quality as a strategy that provides the focus for these five activities is the ongoing process of matching products and services to a real need, which they satisfy. This requires advanced planning.

IDENTIFYING THE NEED

Say, for example, I produce a slide rule. To improve its quality, I must know that the need the product fulfills is hand-held computation. Analysis of competitive products should not be limited to other brands of slide rules, but should include abacuses and calculators, which are also aimed at fulfilling the need for hand-held computation. It would be easy to think that the need is for a slide rule.

The need may be for personal transportation, for making homemade ice cream, for the disposal of garbage, for a pleasant environment in the workplace, for transfer of knowledge, or for the separation of chemical mixtures. The need in the marketplace or in society that the organization intends to fulfill provides the target for the matching and the stability of the strategy. If the strategy is to be sustained over the long term, then the need should be one that will persist over a long period of time.

There are often several products or services in the marketplace at the same time aimed at the same need. Table 1 provides a list of needs and a corresponding product or service intended to fulfill each need. These relationships are not unique and in fact, most of them may be replaced by a dozen other alternatives.

Table 1. Need as a Target for Products and Services

Need	Product or Service
Access to the home	Automatic garage door opener
Transfer of knowledge and promotion of life-long learning	Elementary education
Healthcare	Hospital
Information about important global affairs	Newspaper
Information about demographic patterns	Survey
Separate chemical mixtures on a small scale	High technology filters
Paying routine bills and making purchases	Checking account
Personal transportation	City bus system
Decorative floors (product or service)	Vinyl tile

This need resides in customers and potential customers; customers follow from the need. Potential customers are those who possess the need. There are usually many ways to satisfy a need. For example, in Table 1, automobiles and bicycles may be aimed at the need for personal transportation just as ceramic tile and carpet may be aimed at the need for decorative floor coverings.

It is the responsibility of strategic planning that the organization's statement of purpose articulates the need the organization intends to match, and to plan the development of products or services for, so that the customer may be satisfied. This allows the organization to look beyond its present products and services and provides a vision for innovation. It is usually easier for an organization to list their products and services than to define the need that these products and services are intended to match. The following questions help in defining the need:

What are your current products and services?

How do people use these products or services?

Why should they want them?

What different products or services could be used instead of yours? (This question does not refer to similar products or services offered by competitors.)

In defining the need, there must be a balance between a definition so abstract that it is not useful, and a definition so specific that it leads the organization to believe that the need is for *its* products and services.

DEFINING QUALITY

If quality is to be improved through more precise matching of products and services to a need, then quality must be defined relative to a specific need. This definition of quality consists of a set of measurable characteristics, sometimes called quality characteristics.

Some quality characteristics for hand-held computation are speed, accuracy, complexity of the computation, clarity of display of results, and ease of handling. A distinction should be made between quality characteristics for a need versus a specification for a product or service. For example, a specification for a slide rule might be how easily the center bar slides. On the other hand, the specification for the slide rule may be a predefined numeric accuracy.

Garvin (1987) proposed eight dimensions of quality to help people define quality of products and services. They also can be used to define quality relative to a need. Plesk (1987) and Stamatis (1996) made some modifications to these eight dimensions. Table 2 expands on these dimensions. Some of the additions to the list are merely subheadings under one of Garvin's original dimensions. For example, time could be a subheading under performance. They are listed separately for emphasis and ease of using the list.

Table 2. Dimensions of Quality

Dimension	Meaning
1. Performance	Primary operating characteristics
2. Features	Secondary operating characteristics, added touches
3. Time	Time waiting to get into line, time from concept to production of a new product, time to complete a service
4. Reliability	Extent of failure, free operation over time
5. Durability	Amount of use before replacement is preferable to repair
6. Uniformity	Low variation among repeated outcomes of a process
7. Consistency	Match with documentation, advertising, forecasts, deadlines, or industry standards
8. Serviceability	Resolution of problems and complaints
9. Aesthetics	Characteristics that relate to the senses such as color, fragrance, fit, or finish
10. Personal	Interface characteristics such as punctuality, courtesy, and professionalism
11. Harmless	Characteristics relating to safety, health, or the environment
12. Perceived quality	Indirect measures or inferences about one or more of the dimensions; reputation

To define quality relative to a need, one should develop a list of quality characteristics for the need and then check the list against the dimensions in Table 2 to test for comprehensiveness. A list of quality characteristics for a specific need does not have to contain all of the dimensions in Table 2. Garvin makes the point that to compete on quality, an organization must determine what dimensions are important to the group of customers (segment of the market) on which the organization is focusing. To that, of course, we add that unless appropriate and applicable planning takes place, not much is going to be accomplished. Table 3 contains some quality characteristics for various needs.

Table 3. Quality Characteristics

Need	Quality Characteristics
Decorative flooring	Stain resistance
	Appearance
	Consistency with fashion trends
	Ease of cleaning
	Resistance to scratches
	Time until replacement
	Ease of installation
Pay for routine purchases and bills	Diversity of bills and purchases
	Ease of access to funds
	Security of funds
	Ease of record keeping
	Availability of credit
	Time to make the payment
Healthcare	Extent of prevention of health problems
	Ability to diagnose health problems
	Ability to solve problems
	Personal interface
	concern and caring
	courtesy
	professionalism
	Level of anxiety during treatment
	Duration of treatment
	Access to care

Figure 1—Comparing the quality of four floor products.

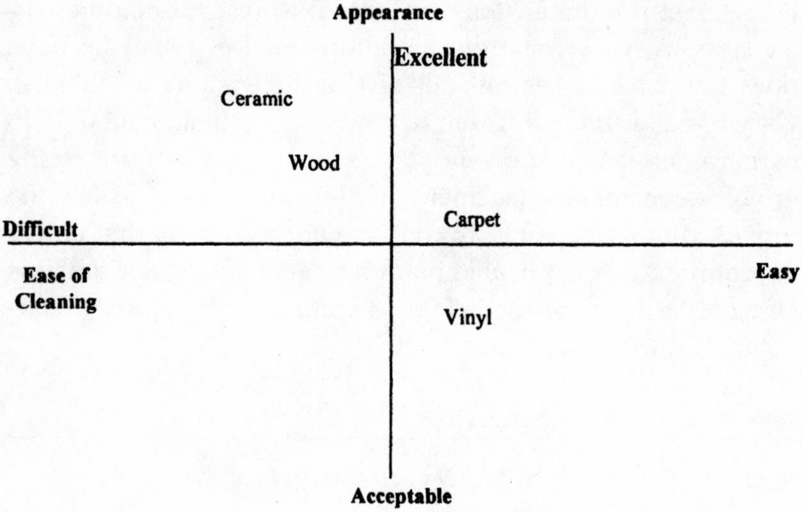

Appearance

Excellent

Ceramic

Wood

Difficult

Carpet

Ease of   Easy
Cleaning

Vinyl

Acceptable

Quality is improved as the match between products or services and the need is improved, which in turn happens the more the match is planned in advance. The degree of matching and planning is determined using the definition of quality. Figure 1 provides an example, comparing the quality of four products, vinyl tile, ceramic tile, carpet, and stained hardwood. Quality is determined by the degree of matching to the need for decorative floors using two quality characteristics: appearance and ease of cleaning.

It is the aim of customer research to understand how different groups of customers define quality. The comparison in Figure 2 could differ widely among different individuals. When performing the matching, the following aspects must be considered:

- Definition of quality will differ among individuals
- Definition of quality will change over time
- An important part of matching is selecting a price
  for the product or service that the customer is willing
  to pay

- In the dynamic environment that we live in, the matching must be ongoing

The foundation of quality as a planning strategy is the continuous matching of products and services to a particular need. Once the need is determined and quality is defined relative to that need, matching of products and services to that need can begin. To successfully perform this ongoing process, the organization must operate as a system. This is the second key element of the planning strategy.

THE ORGANIZATION AS A SYSTEM

A system is an interdependent group of items, people, or processes with a common purpose. Figure 2 depicts an organization as a system. This figure is a slight modification of Deming's production view as a system (Deming, 1986, p.4).

Some important aspects of quality as a strategy that are depicted in this figure include:

- The need is the primary focus and provides the aim for efforts of improvement of quality
- The matching of products and services to the need is ongoing, the system is closed loop
- Suppliers and customers are closely connected to the system
- Customer research and planning are prerequisites for the improvement of quality
- Improvement of quality results from design or redesign of some aspect of the system
- Everyone in the organization should participate in improving quality

Managing the organization as a system is essential to quality as a planning strategy. There are usually fundamental changes to be made in an organization before it actually functions as an integrated system. Many forces promote suboptimization, that is, parts of the organization function without regard for what is best for the entire organization.

Figure 2—The organization viewed as a system.

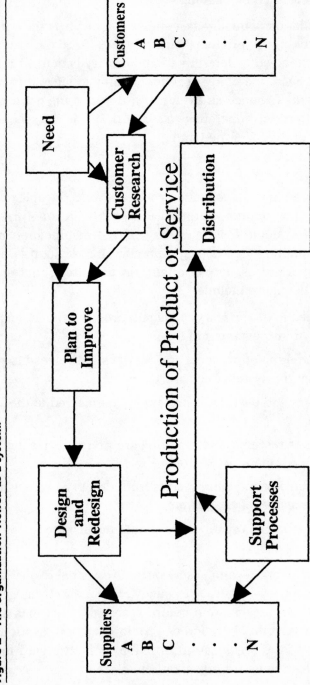

The classic organizational chart itself depicts a group of independent departments rather than a system of linked processes. When the organization is viewed as a system, internal customer/supplier relationships can be identified. The organizational chart depicts the boss as the customer.

Some of the other causes of suboptimization include:

- People not knowing the purpose of the organization and how their work relates to it

- Technical or functional short-sightedness

- Well-intentioned management systems that actually promote short-term thinking or a narrow point of view

- Internal competition

- Optimizing a single measure of success (such as profits) rather than simultaneously optimizing multiple measures of success

Some aids to making the organization perform as a system are discussed below.

CONSTANCY OF PURPOSE

Constancy of purpose is the first, and perhaps most important, of Deming's 14 points. A system has been defined above as an interdependent group of items, people, or processes with a common purpose. If the organization is to function as a system, then everyone in the organization must know what the common purpose of the organization is and how their work contributes to the purpose. This understanding of purpose is facilitated by the development and communication of a statement of purpose. This is the responsibility of the top management of the organization.

There are many ways to articulate the purpose of an organization. A three-part format for a statement of purpose that has been useful in a variety of organizations follows.

1. A mission statement containing the need in society or the marketplace the organization intends to fulfill.

2. A set of beliefs, values, or guiding principles that set the boundaries within which the mission will be accomplished.

3. A vision of how the organization will be structured or will behave in the future to accomplish the mission. (This is particularly important for organizations under-going change.) See Pascarella and Frohman (1989) for some guidance on developing and communicating the purpose of the organization.

Simply stating and communicating the purpose of the organization is not enough to obtain constancy of purpose. Providing the environment is also necessary, so that everyone in the organization can work towards the same purpose and goals. It is easy to get caught up in problems of today and for-get that the long-term existence of the company will depend on allocating resources to the future. These resources are directed at finding better ways to meet the need. Deming points out that improving only operations will not be enough. "It is possible and in fact fairly easy for an organization to go downhill and out of business making the wrong product or offering the wrong type of service, even though everyone in the organization performs with devotion, employing statisti-cal methods and every other aid that can boost efficiency" (Deming, 1986, p.26).

The establishment of constancy of purpose is aided by:

- Communicating within the organization the purpose that this constancy intends to fulfill

- Having this purpose provide the aim for all efforts of improvement

- Allocating resources for research

- Allocating resources for education and training

- Balancing the short-term needs of the organization with long-term improvements in products and services

- Providing opportunity for everyone in the organization to participate in improvements

ORGANIZATION WITHIN THE ORGANIZATION

The foundation of quality as a planning strategy is the ongoing matching of products and services to a need. Anyone possessing the need is a potential customer of the organization. These customers are usually external to the organization. When the organization is viewed as a system, it is easy to see that there are substantial interdependencies among people and departments within an organization. It becomes apparent that there are customer and supplier relationships within an organization. The work of an individual or a group (supplier) is used by another individual or group (customer) in the organization. The two groups are linked in a supplier-customer relationship.

A powerful force against suboptimization is to instill in members of an organization the concept of the internal customer. It aids in alleviating the technical or functional short-sightedness that often results in a disregard for the purpose of the organization.

COOPERATIVE INTERACTION WITH THE OUTSIDE ENVIRONMENT

Organizations are open systems. That is, the environment in which the system (organization) is imbedded has an impact on its performance (von Bertalanffy, 1968). Cooperative interaction with elements of the outside environment provide another means of improving the performance of the organization towards accomplishing its purpose. Cooperation between the organization and its suppliers, its customers, government agencies, and its competitors are opportunities for improvement.

There are interdependencies among different organizations attempting to satisfy the same need with similar products or services. They often share common problems. Cooperation among them is essential, if their approach to satisfying the need is to remain viable; otherwise they will be competing with each other for an increased share of a decreasing market. For example, plastic manufacturers need to cooperate to find ways to reduce their products' environmental toll.

Suppliers are also part of the outside environment. Long-term, mutually beneficial relationships with suppliers are essential. Some aims of a relationship with a supplier are:

- Lower total cost

- Less variation

- Better able to meet the needs of the customer

- Increase in investment for the future

- Decrease in complexity

- Mutually beneficial flow of knowledge

FOCUSING ON MULTIPLE MEASURES OF SUCCESS

A common force for suboptimization of a system is the attempt to define the performance of the system by a single measure. This measure may relate to the entire organization or to a part of the organization. Examples of measures that often function as single measures of success are: profits, return on investment, price of stock, volume of production, percent of legal cases won, scores on standardized tests, and volume of sales.

Given one measure of success, almost any group can be successful in the short-term by optimizing that measure at the expense of other measures. Return on investment can be increased in the short-term by decreasing investment in research and development. Volume of production can be increased by cutting back on preventive maintenance or on tests of new products. Scores on standardized tests can be improved by "teaching for the test."

Optimization of a system results in the improvement of a family of measures of success. Taken as a whole, the measures should be predictors of future success of the company. It is everyones job to contribute to improvement in the family of measures. These measures should relate to a variety of dimensions of the system such as:

- Customers

- Employees

- Business and financial
- Operations
- Outside environment

Table 4 contains some examples of measures in each of these categories.

Table 4. Examples of Measures of Success

CUSTOMERS

Percentage of repeat customers

Warranties, claims, complaints, returns

Key performance characteristics of the product or service
that are global in nature such as:
    percentage of deliveries on time
    scores on standardized tests (school)
    degree of return to normal physical or mental functioning (hospital)
    cycle time, delivery time, completion time, etc.

EMPLOYEES

Level of experience

Level of skills

Turnover

Absenteeism

Measures of inner experience such as the extent to which
people take pride in their work

BUSINESS AND FINANCIAL

Profits

Variance from budget

Share of market

Return on investments

Amount spent on research and development

Amount of resources allocated to the improvement of quality

OPERATIONS

Volume of production

Productivity

Volume of sales

Levels of inventory

Amount of overtime

Amount of scrap or rework

Number of errors

Number of accidents, injuries, or near misses

OUTSIDE ENVIRONMENT

Time allocated to industry groups or advisory groups

Amount of community service

Amount of discharge of pollutants

Number of layoffs

Accidents or injuries related to the product or service

An example is a trucking company that lists the following family of measures as their definition of success:

- Difference between scheduled time of delivery and actual time of delivery
- Accounts receivable over 30 days
- Accidents
- Breakdowns
- Turnover of drivers
- Absenteeism
- Profits

The company believes that improvements in these measures will mean success for the company. It should be noted that the relationships and trade-offs among the different measures in the family are fixed by the present system. Because of the global nature of the measures, no one person or department is solely responsible for an individual measure. It is the responsibility of management to provide leadership for the ongoing matching of products and services to a need in such a way that the entire family of measures is improved. Planning for quality plays a significant role in accomplishing this aim.

Improving the organization's ability to function as a system provides another way to improve quality in addition to the design or redesign of products and processes. Improvement of quality can also be achieved by making changes that affect the system as a whole, such as the establishment of constancy of purpose or the use of the concept of internal customers and suppliers described above.

METHODS TO IMPROVE QUALITY

Thus far, two components have been used to describe quality as a planning strategy: 1) The strategy is based on the ongoing matching of products and services to a need; and 2) This matching is achieved by developing the organization into a system that has as its aim satisfacton of the need that the organization intends to fulfill.

A third element needed to make the strategy viable is a set of methods by which to carry out the improvements in products, processes, or the system as a whole (Fig. 2). Three aspects of the system relating to methods of improving quality are:

1. customer research,

2. planning for quality,

3. the design and redesign of products and processes.

These three aspects provide the link between day-to-day operation of the system and improvement of the system. In organizations in which quality is a strategy, they are well-developed. In organizations in which quality is not yet at the strategic level,

- Customer research is nonexistent, anecdotal, or composed of negative feedback such as complaints or warranty claims

- Planning for quality is nonexistent or separated from business planning

- Emphasis is placed on solving problems or resolving crises rather than making lasting improvements to products and processes

Customer Research

Customer research should focus on the need that the organization intends to fulfill. Relying on negative feedback such as complaints or warranty claims is not sufficient. Present customers will be an important source of information; however, the research should not be limited to them. Anyone possessing the need the organization intends to fulfill is a source of information. The aims of customer research are to:

- Identify those possessing the need (identify the market)

- Stratify those who possess the need into groups (segment the market)

- Define quality relative to the need for each segment using measurable characteristics

- Assist in monitoring quality of present products and services
- Improve the relationship with customers

The following are some methods to be considered for use in customer research:

- Informal conversation
- Written surveys
- Personal interviews
- Group interviews
- Observation of people possessing the need
- Trading places with people possessing the need
- Product market tests
- Observations by field engineers at your customer's facilities
- Quality function deployment (QFD)

PLANNING FOR QUALITY

When quality is an organizational strategy, strategic planning and business planning include planning of activities to improve quality.

Inputs to the plan include:

- The statement of purpose of the organization
- The organization viewed as a system of linked processes
- Customer research
- Other information relevant to the need the organization intends to fulfill, such as new technology, new government regulations, or changes in the business environment
- Information from suppliers
- Information from those in the organization, especially with regard to processes most in need of improvement

Outcomes of the plan include:

- Guidance on an overall method to reach the objective
- Charters for activities of individuals or teams aimed at improving quality
- Roles and responsibilities of people involved in improvements
- Allocation of resources
- Assessment of the need for training

There are many different methods for developing a plan for quality. One process for planning that uses the inputs listed above to produce the outcomes that are listed consists of the following steps suggested by Hardaker and Ward (1987):

1. Develop strategic objectives
2. Relate strategic objectives to new or existing products or processes
3. Set priorities for improvement
4. Match resources to the priorities
5. Develop charters for design or redesign of products or processes

METHODS FOR THE DESIGN AND REDESIGN OF PRODUCTS AND PROCESSES

Improvement of quality should not be confused with solving problems or "fire fighting." Solving problems, although necessary for most organizations, simply maintains the status quo. Lasting improvements come from design or redesign of processes or products or changes to the system as a whole.

Although improvements in quality result from change, all change does not result in improvement. Changes that result in the improvement of quality come from people with increased knowledge of the system and appropriate planning up front. A model for the improvement of quality based on learning was

Figure 3—Model to improve quality based on learning.

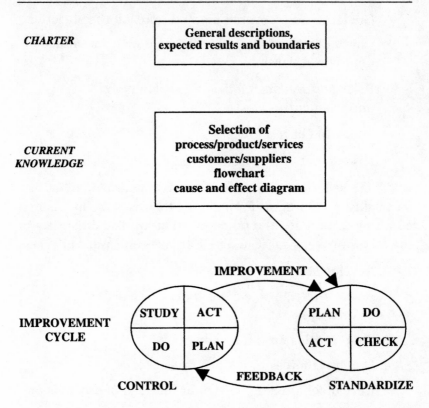

introduced by Moen and Nolan (1987) and is modified in Figure 3 to include the cycle of feedback.

The first component of the model is to define a charter for the team or individual. The charter will provide guidance to the team and will help them with many of the decisions that will need to be made during the life of the team.

The second component is a summary of the current knowledge of the team. At this stage, the team documents its knowledge of:

- The needs of the customer
- The processes or products that are related to the team's charter
- How the selected process or product works

- The relationship betwen cause and effect
- The important quality characteristics

To improve quality, a significant amount of time will be spent increasing the team's knowledge. This new knowledge will then be used to develop an improvement. To gain this knowledge and make the improvements, a series of improvement cycles are performed. Variations of this cycle have been called the Shewhart Cycle, Deming Cycle, plan-do-check (study) -act (PDCA) cycle, and advanced quality planning.

The improvement cycle has four phases. First, a plan is developed to increase knowledge of the product or process, possibly by testing a change. Second, the plan is carried out. Next, the data is studied and conclusions are drawn. Finally, a decision is made as to whether the current state of knowledge is sufficient to take action on the product or process or whether another cycle is needed. This model provides the framework within which to apply statistical or other methods to develop and implement improvements. Some of these methods will be discussed throughout the book.

People in the organization who are planning the activities or who are working to make the improvements need to be able to visualize work as a process and to visualize the organization as a system of linked processes. It is usually easy to think of manufacturing as a process but difficult to think of new product development, forecasting, budgeting, or planning capital expenditures as processes.

Statistical methods such as control charts, Pareto analysis, scatter diagrams, and planned experiments will be useful for determining cause and effect relationships related to products and processes. Flowcharts and cause and effect (fishbone) diagrams are useful for summary of the team's current knowledge that is relevant to their charter.

Knowledge of variation and its causes is essential to the improvement of quality. Reduction of variation will often be an important source of improvement. Variation in products, processes, or among people's performance is a result of two types of causes. *Common causes* of variation are those causes that are inherent in the process over time, affect everyone working in the process, and affect all outcomes of the process. *Special causes* of variation are those causes that are not part of the process all of the time or do not affect everyone, but arise because of specific circumstances.

The responsibility for improvement and the methods of improvement will differ depending on whether common or special causes dominate. Fundamental change is usually needed when common causes dominate and this change is the responsibility of management. On the other hand, improvements to eliminate special causes and those responsible for the improvements will depend on the specific circumstances that resulted in the special cause. (As a general rule, the corrections are usually at the place the special cause occurred and corrected by those closest to the process and those who have ownership of the process.) Control charts are used to determine if the variation is a result of common or special causes. See Nolan and Provost (1990) for more information on the subject of variation.

Because of the interdependencies in a system, many improvements will come from the efforts of cross-functional teams. Basic skills related to conducting meetings, obtaining balanced participation in teams, resolving conflicts, and making decisions in teams will be needed (see Scholtes, 1988).

LEADERSHIP TO CARRY OUT THE STRATEGY

The three basic elements of a strategy based on quality have been discussed: 1) The aim is ongoing matching of products and services to a need; 2) This matching is achieved by developing an organization that performs as a system with the need as the target; and 3) A set of methods to insure that changes result in the improvement of quality.

However, this strategy can not simply be installed or implemented like a new computer system in an organization. There is a need for knowledgeable leadership to carry out the strategy and make it successful.

"The aim of leadership should be to improve the performance of man and machine, to improve quality, to increase output, and simultaneously to bring pride of workmanship to people." (Deming, 1986, p.248) To accomplish this aim, a leader will need knowledge in a wide variety of areas. Deming (1989) describes the body of knowledge that is necessary for leadership as "profound knowledge." This body of knowledge contains knowledge of a system; statistical theory, especially the theory of variation; the theory of knowledge; and psychology. A leader does not need to be an expert in all of these areas but should know something about each, how the different areas interrelate, and why they are important for the improvement of quality. For a more detailed discussion of this area, see Stamatis (1997).

Intrinsically motivating people to improve the system and its products is one of the tasks of a leader. This intrinsic motivation comes from:

- A belief that the purpose of the organization is worthwhile

- A system that allows people to enjoy their work and take pride in its outcomes

- An environment that encourages improvement by providing the time for people to participate in improving the system

- Recognition and appreciation of efforts

As intrinsic motivation is increased there will be less reliance on outside or extrinsic motivation such as bonuses, awards, competition, and the trappings of success. Reliance on an extrinsic motivation often promotes short-term thinking and competition. The extrinsic motivation diverts attention and energy from the purpose of the organization; attaining the extrinsic reward becomes the goal.

Someone exercising leadership is probably generating disequilibrium rather than keeping things on an even keel (Heifitz, 1988). While fundamental change requires disequilibrium, without leadership this disequilibrium can be destructive. There must be a plan and a role model to follow. There must be leadership by example. Deming (1990) lists the following attributes of a quality leader at any level in the organization:

- Has constancy of purpose
- Understands how the work of his or her group supports the purpose of the organization
- Focuses on the needs of the customer, both internal and external
- Is coach and counsel, not judge
- Removes obstacles to pride in work
- Understands variation (avoids tampering)
- Is willing to take risks
- Works to improve the system
- Creates an atmosphere of trust and support
- Forgives a mistake
- Knows his or her limitations and continues to improve

To this list, we add that the person supplying leadership for quality must know and practice the principles of advanced quality planning. This book is devoted to the discussion of advanced quality planning.

REFERENCE

Deming, W. Edwards. *Out of the Crisis.* Cambridge, MA: Massachusetts Institute of Technology. Center for Advanced Engineering Study, 1986.

Deming, W. Edwards. "Foundation for Management of Quality in the Western World." Unpublished paper from his 4 day seminar, 1990.

Garvin, David A. "Competing on the Eight Dimensions of Quality." *Harvard Business Review* (November, 1987).

Hardaker, Maurice, and Ward, Bryan. "Getting Things Done." *Harvard Business Review* (November-December, 1987).

Heifetz, Ronald. "Interview on Leadership." *INC* (October, 1988).

Kohn, Alfie. *No Contest-The Case Against Competition.* New York, NY: Houghton Mifflin Company, 1986.

Moen, Ronald D., and Nolan, Thomas W. "Process Improvement." *Quality Progress* (September, 1987).

Nolan, Thomas W., and Provost, Lloyd P. "Understanding Variation." *Quality Progress* (May, 1990).

Pascarella, Perry, and Frohman, Mark. *The Purpose-Driven Organization.* San Francisco, CA: Jossey-Bass Inc., 1989.

Plesk, Paul E. "Defining Quality at the Marketing/Development Interface." *Quality Progress* (June, 1987).

President's Commission on Industrial Competitiveness. (1985). *Global Competition-The New Reality.* Volume I. Washington D.C.: U.S. Government Printing Office, 1985.

Scholtes, Peter R. *The Team Handbook.* Madison, WI: Joiner Associates, 1988.

Stamatis, D.H. *TQM Engineering Handbook.* Marcel Dekker, Inc. NY, NY, 1997.

Stamatis, D.H. *Total Quality Service.* Delray Beach, FL: St. Lucie Press, 1996.

von Bertalanffy, Ludwig. *General System Theory.* New York, NY: George Braziller, Inc., 1968.

TWO

Overview of Advanced Quality Planning (AQP)

WHY USE AQP?

Before we address the "why" of planning, we assume that things do go wrong. But why do they go wrong? Obviously, there are many specific answers that address this question. Often the answer falls into one of these four categories:

- We never have enough time, so things are omitted
- We have done this, this way, so we minimize the effort
- We assume that we know what has been requested, so we do not listen carefully
- We assume that because we finish a project, improvement will indeed follow, so we bypass the improvement steps

In essence then, the customer appears satisfied, but a product, service, or process is not improved at all. This is precisely why it is imperative for organizations to look at quality planning as a totally integrated activity that involves the entire organization. The organization must expect changes in its operations by employing cross-functional and multi-disciplinary teams to exceed customer desires—not just meet requirements. A quality plan includes, but is not limited to:

- A team to manage the plan
- Timing to monitor progress
- Procedures to define operating policies
- Standards to clarify requirements
- Controls to stay on course
- Data and feedback to verify and to provide direction
- Action plan to initiate change

Advanced quality planning, then, is a methodology that yields a quality plan for the creation of a process, product, or service consistent with customer requirements. It allows for maximum quality in the workplace by planning and documenting the process of improvement. AQP is the essential discipline that offers both the customer and the supplier a systematic approach to quality planning, to defect prevention, and to continual improvement. Some specific uses are:

- In the auto industry demand is so high that Chrysler, Ford, and General Motors have developed a standardized approach to AQP. That standardized approach is a requirement for the QS-9000 certification. In addition, each company has its own way of measuring success in the implementation and reporting phase of AQP tasks.
- Auto suppliers are expected to demonstrate the ability to participate in early design activities from concept through prototype and on to production.
- Quality planning is initiated as early as possible, well before print release.

- Planning for quality is needed particularly when a company's management establishes a policy of "prevention" as opposed to "detection."

- When you use advanced quality planning, you provide for the organization and resources needed to accomplish the quality improvement task.

- Early planning prevents waste (scrap, rework, and repair), identifies required engineering changes, improves timing for new product introduction, and lowers costs.

WHEN DO WE USE AQP?

We use AQP when we need to meet or exceed expectations in the following situations:

- During the development of new processes and products

- Prior to changes in processes and products

- When reacting to processes or products with reported quality concerns

- Before tooling is transferred to new producers or new plants

- Prior to process or product changes affecting product safety or compliance to regulations

In the case of an automotive supplier, the supplier is to maintain evidence of the use of defect prevention techniques prior to production launch. The defect prevention methods used are to be implemented as soon as possible in the new product development cycle.

It follows then, that the basic requirements for appropriate and complete AQP are:

1. Team approach

2. Systematic development of products/services and processes

3. Reduction in variation (this must be done, even before the customer requests improvement of any kind)

4. Development of a control plan

As AQP is continuously used in a given organization, the obvious need for its implementation becomes stronger and stronger. That need may be demonstrated through:

- Minimizing the present level of problems and errors
- Yielding a methodology that integrates customer and supplier development activities as well as concerns
- Exceeding present reliability/durability levels to surpass the competition's and customer's expectations
- Reinforcing the integration of quality tools with the latest management techniques for total improvement
- Exceeding the limits set for cycle time and delivery time
- Developing new and improving existing methods of communicating the results of quality processes for a positive impact throughout the organization

WHAT IS THE DIFFERENCE BETWEEN AQP AND APQP?

AQP is the generic methodology for all quality planning activities in all industries. APQP is AQP; however, it emphasizes the product orientation of quality. APQP is used specifically in the automotive industry. In this book, both terms are used interchangeably.

How Do We Make AQP Work?

There are no guarantees for making AQP work. However, there are three basic characteristics that are essential and must be adhered to for AQP to work. They are:

1. Activities must be measured based on *who, what, where,* and *when.*

2. Activities must be tracked based on shared information (*how* and *why*), as well as work schedules and objectives.

3. Activities must be focused on the goal of quality-cost-delivery, using information and consensus to improve quality.

As long as our focus is on the triad of quality-cost-delivery, AQP can produce positive results. After all, we all need to reduce cost while we increase quality and reduce lead time. That is the focus of an AQP program and the more we understand it, the more likely we are going to have a workable plan.

ARE THERE PITFALLS IN PLANNING?

Just like everything else, planning has pitfalls. However, if one considers the alternatives, there is no doubt that planning will win out by far. To be sure, perhaps one of the greatest pitfalls in *planning* is the lack of support by management and a hostile climate for its practice. So, the question is not really whether there are any pitfalls, but why such support is quite often withheld and why such climates do arise in organizations that claim to be "quality oriented"?

Some specific pitfalls in any planning environment may have to do with commitment, time allocation, objective interpretations, tendency toward conservatism, and an obsession with control. All these elements breed a climate of conformity and inflexibility that favors incremental changes for the short term, but ignore the potential of large changes in the long run. Of these, the most misunderstood element is commitment.

The assumption is that with the support of management, all will be well. This assumption is based in the axiom of F. Taylor at the turn of the 20th century, which is, "there is one best way." Planning is assumed to generate the one best way not only to formulate, but to implement, a particular idea, product, and so on. Sometimes, this notion is not correct. In today's "agile world" we must be prepared to evaluate several alternatives of equal value.

As a consequence, the issue is not simply whether management is committed to planning. It is also, as Mintzberg (1994) has observed, 1) whether planning is committed to management, 2) commitment to planning engenders commitment to the process of strategy making, to the strategies that result from that process, and ultimately to the taking of effective actions by the organization, and 3) whether the very nature of planning actually fosters managerial commitment to itself.

Another pitfall, of equal value, is the cultural attitude of "fighting fires." In most organizations, we reward problem solvers rather than planners. As a consequence, in most organizations the emphasis is on low risk "fire fighting," when in fact it should be on planning a course of action that will be realistic, productive, and effective. Planning may be tedious in the early stages of conceptual design, but it is certainly less expensive and much more effective than corrective action in the implementation stage of any product or service development.

DO WE REALLY NEED ANOTHER QUALITATIVE TOOL TO GAGE QUALITY?

While quantitative methods are excellent ways to address the "who," "what," "when," and "where," qualitative study focuses on the "why." It is in this "why" that the focus of advanced quality planning contributes the most results, especially in the exploratory-feasibility-phase of our projects.

So, the answer to the question is a categorical "yes," because the aim of qualitative study is to understand rather than to measure, it is used to increase knowledge, clarify issues, define problems, formulate hypotheses, and generate ideas. Using qualitative methodology in advanced quality planning endeavors will indeed lead to a more holistic, empathetic customer portrait than can be achieved through quantitative study, which, in turn, can lead to enlightened engineering and production decisions as well as advertisement campaigns.

HOW DO WE USE THE QUALITATIVE METHODOLOGY IN AN ADVANCED QUALITY PLANNING SETTING?

Since this book focuses on the applicability of tools rather than on the details of the tools, the methodology is summarized in seven steps:

BEGIN WITH THE END IN MIND. This may be obvious; however, it is how most goals are achieved. This is the stage where the experimenter determines how the study results will be implemented: What courses of action can the customer take and how will they be influenced by the study results? Clearly understanding the goal defines the study problem and report structure. To ensure implementation, determine what the report should look like and what it should contain.

DETERMINE WHAT'S IMPORTANT. All resources are limited and therefore we cannot do everything. However, we can do the most important things. We must learn to use the Pareto principle (vital few as opposed to the trivial many). To identify what is important, we have many methods, including asking about advantages and disadvantages, benefits desired, likes and dislikes, importance ratings, preference regression, key driver analysis, conjoint and discrete choice analysis, force field analysis, value analysis, and many others. The focus of these approaches is to improve performance in areas in which a competitor is ahead or in areas where your organization is determined to hold the lead in a particular product and or service.

USE SEGMENTATION STRATEGIES. Not everyone wants the same thing. Learn to segment markets for specific products and/or services that deliver value to your customer. By segmenting based on *wants*, the engineering and product development can develop action-oriented recommendations for specific markets, and therefore contribute to customer satisfaction.

USE ACTION STANDARDS. To be successful, standards must be used, but with diagnostics. Standards must be defined at the outset. They are always considered as the minimum requirements. Then when the results come in, there will be an identified action to be taken, even if it is to do nothing. List the possible results and the corresponding actions that could be taken for each. Diagnostics, on the other hand, provides the "what if" questions that one considers in pursuing the standards. Usually, they provide alternatives through a set of questions, specific to the standard. If you cannot list actions, then you have not designed an actionable study. Better design it again.

<u>DEVELOP OPTIMALS</u>. Everyone wants to be the best. The problem with this statement is that there is only room for one best. All other choices are second best. When an organization focuses on being the best in everything, that organization is asking for a failure. No one can be the best in everything and sustain it. What we can do is focus on the optimal combination of choices. By doing so, we usually have a usable recommendation based on a course of action that is reasonable and within the constraints of the organization.

<u>GIVE GRASP-AT-A-GLANCE RESULTS</u>. The focus of any study is to turn people into numbers (wants into requirements), numbers into a story (requirements into specifications), and that story into action (specifications into products or services). But the story must be easy to understand. The results must be clear and well-organized so that they and their implications can be grasped at a glance.

<u>RECOMMEND CLEARLY</u>. Once you have a basis for an action, recommend that action clearly. You do not want a doctor to order tests and then hand you the laboratory report. You want to be told what is wrong and how to fix it. From an advanced quality planning perspective, we want the same. That is, we want to know where the bottlenecks are, what kind of problems we will encounter, and how we will overcome them for a successful delivery.

REFERENCE

Mintzberg, H. (1994). *The Rise and Fall of Strategic Planning*. New York, NY: Free Press, 1994.

THREE

Team Building

Teams are becoming an accepted way of operating. As a company seeks to make any kind of improvement or start a quality initiative, including advanced quality procedures, team building becomes a requirement. A company, whether an original equipment manufacturer (OEM) or a supplier, is expected to initiate and develop internal cross-functional and multi-disciplinary teams for launches of new or changed products. The newly formed team is expected to use quality planning techniques, and is to be proactive throughout the development and launch of products. Pro-activity is mandatory, rather than waiting to "fix" things after the fact.

A cross-functional team should usually include design, manufacturing, and quality engineers, production, purchasing, and other personnel. Suppliers are urged to include their customer's purchasing, quality, and product engineering personnel on their quality planning teams.

THE ISSUE OF CULTURE AND TEAMS

In the past, most organizations dealt with problems as they occurred. Today, however, intensified competition requires us to move faster. Organizations must recognize that their internal structure may have to change to facilitate new learning, as well as new technologies and even new processes.

By definition, organizational culture is the set of values, often taken for granted, that help people in an organization understand which actions are considered acceptable and which are considered unacceptable. Values, on the other hand, are often communicated through symbolic means.

One of the derivatives of culture change is the way an organization deals with teams and their effectiveness. To be sure, a team must be empowered (given authority and responsibility) to take control of an opportunity to resolve an existing or even a potential issue. An effective empowerment may include the following:

- Give employees freedom to do tasks their own way within prescribed limits
- Mutually agree on results and performance
- Encourage employees to define, implement, and communicate progress on tasks
- Entrust employees with complete projects and tasks
- Explain relevance to larger projects and organizational goals
- Give employees the authority necessary to complete tasks
- Provide proper training and guidance
- Delegate on basis of employee interest whenever possible

The results of an appropriately empowered team will be commensurable with at least some of the following characteristics internal to the team itself:

- Individual roles
- Team norms and expectations
- Conformity
- Leadership
- Team cohesiveness
- Team size
- Synergism

For the team results to mean anything, the goals of the team must be defined up front as early as possible with the following characteristics, which spell out the acronym SMART:

They must be Specific

They must be Measurable

They must be Assignable

They must be Realistic

They must be Time Bound

In addition, both the goals and the target outcomes of any team activity must be decided by consensus. Otherwise, the goals and decisions reached will be questionable and the implementation may suffer.

REASONS FOR BUILDING AN AQP TEAM

When a company establishes a cross-functional team with the necessary planning and process/product knowledge in the required technical disciplines, they also imply a strong company commitment to providing the time and authority to the team developing and skill to implement the program. Building a team will accomplish the following:

1. Team building allows an organization to reduce or eliminate myopia during the critical path planning period, by providing a multiple point of view. The introduction of different individuals who have diversified job functions and experiences will increase the synergy and, therefore, generate a better resolution. The team leader seeks out the individual, and he or she is encouraged to contribute his or her experience and skills to finding the problems and solutions in the development of a product or process.

2. Team building allows for group ownership of a product or process. Functional ownership of product or process development limits the time/phase perspective. By involving employees of all levels, team ownership is established. The long-term benefit is that the owner-

ship lasts beyond the introduction life of the product
or process.

3. Team building allows for the brilliance of different disciplines and functions to enter into your product and
   process development. Diversity breeds success.

4. Team building allows for synergy and an expansion of
   the concepts, with multi-discipline input. When a team
   brings varied perspectives to a problem, it will result in
   solutions being revealed that would otherwise be hidden. This is especially valuable early on. Problems that
   the team solves prior to print release are design
   changes. After the print release, changes can be much
   more costly to the organization. Problems the team
   identifies and solves in the early stages of product
   development will have an average return on your
   investment of 1:10 return ratio.

5. Team building allows the organization to spread out
   the workload. AQP is a big program, so each part of
   your organization should share the workload and the
   burden as well as the rewards.

6. Finally, team building allows the employees to feel
   ownership in the firm, by being involved in planning
   the company's future. The results are involved, con-
   cerned, and happy employees.

Because the process of AQP is broad and involves many
individuals from both customer and supplier bases, conflict
invariably occurs. When that happens, the following alternatives to resolve the conflict may be of use.

Resolution is used when conflict has become disruptive,
too much time and effort are spent on conflict rather than on
productive efforts, and conflict focuses on internal goals of the
team rather than on organizational goals.

Stimulation is used when work teams are stagnant and
comfortable with the status quo, consensus among team
members is too easily reached, teams are not creative or moti-
vated to challenge traditional ideas, and change within the
organization is needed to remain competitive.

Team Development

Any team goes through several stages. Typically these stages are:

orientation

redefinition

coordination

formalization

In team formation, differentiation and definition of the core team and the extended team should be done early. The core team is responsible for the majority of problems, often on a daily basis. On the other hand, the extended team will be used on an "as needed" basis for special concerns and questions. The extended team serves as a resource group to the core team. It must be recognized that both the core and the extended team are dynamic and, over time and in some cases, their composition may be changed. A typical graphical presentation of both teams is viewed in Figure 4.

Team positions typically include team leader, recorder, participants, AQP coordinator, facilitator, and note taker.

Figure 4—A typical APQP team.

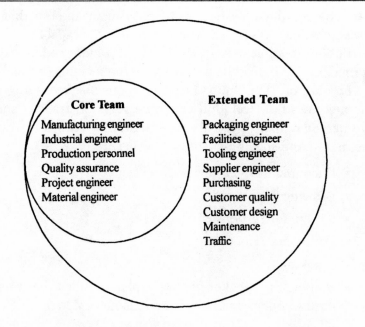

Core Team

Manufacturing engineer
Industrial engineer
Production personnel
Quality assurance
Project engineer
Material engineer

Extended Team

Packaging engineer
Facilities engineer
Tooling engineer
Supplier engineer
Purchasing
Customer quality
Customer design
Maintenance
Traffic

Team leader: This individual is responsible for bringing together all the owners of the problem/concern and is most likely the person with accountability for resolving issues.

Recorder: This individual is responsible for recording all pertinent information discussed and acts as a time keeper.

Participants: These are the individual members of the team assigned specific tasks and responsibilities for the project. To be an effective team member one must have:

- Interest in the project
- Knowledge of the project
- Identification with the project
- Authority to get things done
- Skills to develop and implement the results
- Knowledge of the product's reliability and durability, and the customer's expectation
- Knowledge of potential problems in productivity and quality
- Knowledge of typical problems associated with the project and their solution

AQP Coordinator: This individual oversees the team's activities. The coordinator's responsibility is to make sure that the goals, schedules, resources, and personnel are available and that restrictions to implementing the results are addressed. It is quite normal for this individual not to attend the meetings regularly.

Facilitator: This individual is responsible for seeing that the meetings flow well and everyone stays on track. Usually, this person remains neutral and sees that the team's objectives are met. Some specific facilitation skills are:

- Encouraging open discussion
- Drawing people out
- Calling for responses
- Deliberate refocusing
- Tracking
- Helping the speaker further explain an idea that was hard to understand or that needs more detail

- Preserving the focus of the discussion while encouraging participation from new speakers
- Keeping two or three speakers from monopolizing the discussion
- Keeping track of various lines of thought
- Paraphrasing the speaker's statement and then asking open-ended questions. Example: It sounds like you were saying, "most people are uneasy with change." Can you give me an example of what you mean? You were saying, "to wait 6 weeks before we sign the contract." Say more about that.

NOTE: Do not ask the team which item they would like to focus on first. It will mire the team down talking about what to talk about.

Note Taker: This individual collects, catalogues, and files all documentation needed by the team and provides materials (as needed) for each team meeting.

How Is the AQP Coordinator Appointed?

The selection of an individual who will be responsible for guiding the AQP program from program release through product launch is critical. The probability is high that if the company is one that launches many products, then you will have an AQP specialist, facilitator, or coordinator available. If you have an outside consultant, you must have a team leader from your company available at all times to coordinate and steer the program.

The selected coordinator should have the ability to guide, direct, motivate, train, and support the team. The following responsibilities are assumed by the appointed AQP coordinator or leader:

1. To provide leadership when required—to direct the team meetings and assist in guiding the team in setting their goals and objectives
2. To provide the team the needed support and resources with backup from the top management
3. To provide the team with a method to evaluate progress toward the team's goals and objectives

4. To establish the team meeting agendas, times, and location

5. To provide for the recording of the meeting notes and the publication and the distribution of those minutes. A recorder may be appointed to aid with this chore and the logistics of conducting the team meetings.

In addition, the coordinator or leader should monitor the team to ensure that the team members are open to all ideas presented and respect the consensus of the team's resolutions. The impartiality of the coordinator or leader to the team's decision making is the cornerstone of the team's success in AQP.

How Do We Assemble the Team?

The number and structure of the design/process or production/process teams a company uses depend on the company's size and number of products it introduces each year. The design product/process team eventually evolves into a production product/process team.

When designing or producing a product/process, two teams are used, a core team and an extended team. These two teams change in membership in response to the introduction and design of a new product/process or to changes in product/process. In essence, over time and depending on the specific situations, both teams may change members.

The core team remains constant in the short-term, and the expanded team contains specialists who meet with the team in response to the team's special needs. The core and extended teams function together at various times. In either case, both core and extended teams are driven by the needs of the initial product/process's design concept right through to the process's production launch at job 1. At this point, the design team evolves into the production product/process team. The core and extended teams are changed in response to this evolution.

The Core Team

The core team is appointed as a permanent component of the overall team structure. The core team should ideally have four to six members. A team consisting of more than this number will result in mass meetings, confusing agreements, chaotic discussions, mini agendas, and personal issues, and the consensus decision will be very difficult to obtain. If the core team members are properly selected, all needed decisions will flow from the smaller sized group. The power of their decision, of course, is based on the notion of synergy.

The core team members are the foundation of the *design or production* team. The initial AQP team remains with the product's *design* development from concept to "feasibility approval" and print release. When the organization first conceives the new product or process, the first team selected to conduct and implement the AQP procedures is the core design product/process team. Later, when production of the new product begins, the team will progress into a production product/process team, which will continue the quest for continuing improvement of the product.

The Extended Team

The core team expands to include members who are specialists and may contribute specific knowledge to the core team. These individuals are asked to participate in specific product design and development studies or production and manufacturing product process "continuing" improvement studies, where their knowledge and expertise are recognized as an added advantage. When information pertaining to their specialty is needed, extended team members are invited to team meetings to contribute. When their portion of the function is complete, they return to their original job assignments.

For example: A purchasing individual may be needed for a specific input regarding a supplier issue. His/Her participation is very important to the decision. However, as soon as this individual's contribution has been recognized and taken into consideration for the decision, then this individual is free to return to his/her normal duties.

The core and extended team meetings should not have more than 10 team members. Limit topics for the agenda or use subgroup meetings when necessary. This is especially true if the project is complex and very large.

Design Core Team Members

The core design team member should be selected from among the following people:

Design or product engineer. This individual is capable of contributing the management knowledge for the design product/process activities, because, as a general rule, all future product/process decisions are related to the product/process design. The individual who understands this product/process design best should manage the development of the product.

Quality assurance representative. This individual is capable of contributing the link with historical and performance data. In addition, this individual is frequently familiar with sales returns and warranty data.

Finance or cost representative. This individual is capable of contributing the knowledge of product/process costs. A finance or cost representative is not necessary if you already have a realistic cost assessment, and your total program will not be put in jeopardy due to poor cost projection.

Industrial engineer. This individual is capable of contributing the knowledge of an appropriate product/design flow, labor standards, and machine capacity studies.

Safety compliance representative. This individual is capable of contributing the knowledge of compliance with OSHA and CAFE standards and monetary or legal liability dictated by the government. In addition, this individual should be aware of the ergonomic and legal requirements, as they effect the workplace and product safety standards.

Material engineer. This individual is capable of contributing the knowledge for selecting materials for the product.

Sales engineer. This individual is capable of contributing the "voice of the customer" with regard to their particular needs.

Manufacturing engineer. This individual is capable of contributing the knowledge for determining if the product can be made as designed.

Extended Design Team Members

Although the following list is not the absolute list for selecting the extended members, the following specialists should be considered a starting point. They may well provide information that proves valuable to the design.

Supplier quality assurance (SQA) representative. This individual assists in the decision as to who will supply raw materials. SQA is a liaison with your supplier base and is used to decide what suppliers to use.

Supplier manufacturing engineer. This individual assists with appropriate design selections.

Purchasing representative. This individual, working in tandem with the SQA representative, assists in determining your total cost package and your selection of appropriate suppliers.

Materials control. This individual assists in your program planning and your material needs projections that are essential to costing your program.

Service engineer. This individual assists in the "design for service" that is becoming recognized as an important segment in the organization's expectations for profit. If the product cannot be serviced in the field, long-term sales will suffer. "Design for service" is based on the assumption that dissatisfied customers tell others about their dissatisfaction at a higher rate than do satisfied customers.

Traffic/packaging. This individual assists in packaging design to optimize the logistics for the product. Their contribution depends upon the product/process. How the specific product is packaged and how this product gets to market is as important to the overall *program cost* as are other strategic decisions. Also, this individual should have some knowledge of customs regulations, if the product is going to cross international boarders.

Core Production/Process Team Members

The job of the core production/process team is to develop plans and activities that culminate in the launch and continuing production of products that are error free and satisfy the organization's customers. The core production team membership may be selected from among the following people:

Manufacturing or process engineer or your project manager. This individual contributes to the task of fielding your

machine, process, or product. The engineer is normally selected because the function of engineering in most companies is to:

- Purchase production hardware
- Design the production facility
- Work with the design/or product engineer, select the appropriate materials to make the product
- Write the Process Sheets
- Select and purchase workers' tools
- Design work stations
- Determine ambient atmosphere that product will be fabricated in
- Write build of materials (BOM) for product
- Develop repair methods

Industrial engineer. This individual contributes to the
work station management knowledge and determines the
most efficient work methods.

Salaried worker who is normally the supervisor. This
individual contributes his knowledge of fabricating the prod-
uct/ process or machine.

Production worker. This individual contributes production-
level process knowledge to the development of your product.

Quality engineer. This individual contributes the knowledge of historical data about your process/machine, the accuracy and validity of the data available for your past
production, your customer warranty, and your sales returns
and the development of your product "acceptance standards,"
which will reduce your random rejection of parts.

Materials control representative. This individual contributes information on and evaluation of the raw material purchases and determines the in-house material availability.

Extended Production/Process Team Members

The following personnel may be considered for the extended
production/process team membership:

Maintenance person. This individual contributes knowledge of the technical requirements for machinery, time allocation for equipment/or process installation, and maintenance requirements.

Laboratory test engineer. This individual contributes knowledge of the tests required by the customer or government for the new product. Also, this individual may help in determining which facility to use to perform the tests.

Lay-out technician. This individual contributes the knowledge of the organization's approach to product lay-out or to expedite the needed changes for the process/product.

Cost accounting representative. This individual contributes knowledge of cost projections. If this person is knowledgeable about activity based costing (ABC), so much the better.

Supplier personnel. This individual contributes knowledge of the suppliers' control plans and the individual suppliers' problems, which may include meeting program cost and time constraints.

Customer quality assurance representative. This individual contributes to customer familiarity with the company. Furthermore, it gives the customer a sense of ownership and understanding of the firm's problems and solutions.

HOW DO WE USE THE TEAM EFFECTIVELY?

Much has been written about teams (Sholtes, 1989; Moran et al., 1996; Roming, 1996; Robbins, 1974, and many others), their organization, and their effectiveness. It is not my function to do an exhaustive study on how to make the team effort effective, rather, it is my intent to give the reader direction in understanding how the team may be effective in an AQP environment. Perhaps the starting point that determines the effectiveness of any team is understanding its mission. A good start is to review the mission statement (or charter of the team). The following are some questions to guide the team:

Is the mission (charter) statement

- Clear?
- Concise?
- Consistent?

- Focused on the team purpose?
- Easy to understand?

Does the mission (charter) statement:

- Provide direction for goals, objectives, performance standards?
- Specify products and/or services that the team will provide?
- Address the customer's needs?
- Include vision, ambition, and stretch?

Once the mission is understood by all members, then the next step for the team is to address the following questions. These questions will contribute to effectiveness in the AQP team environment.

- Do team members have an understanding of advanced quality planning techniques?

- Do the team members (core and expanded) have appropriate and applicable training in: 1) team building, 2) problem-solving methodologies, 3) group dynamics, and 4) consensus building, for key members or all members?

Is there a procedure or schedule for the following:

- Holding meetings. Establish consistent meeting times and a place to meet.
- Reporting results internally. Each team meeting should result in published minutes to designated participating members.
- Reporting results externally. A cycle of reporting should be established early on and then followed. For example: Every three months, communication should be established with external interests and particularly top management.
- Monitoring and reporting progress.
- Does the core team membership include at least four members from the areas recommended in this book?
- Is there a consensus on the team's objectives and goals?

Connecting With Other Teams

AQP team members must come in contact with other teams inside the organization as well as outside of it. The following guidelines provide a structure for making an effective connection.

ASK FOR HELP

New teams: Ask for help from established teams regarding:

mission (charter) statement

ground rules

agendas

meeting minutes

process for working effectively with other teams

All teams: Look for other teams that

have already solved problems you are facing

are contributing to your difficulties

will be affected later by what you are doing

ANALYZE YOUR TEAM

- What does your team have in common with other teams?
- Is it possible to accomplish a shared objective with another team?
- Are there overlapping or redundant tasks among teams?
- Will a joint project accomplish objectives more quickly?
- How is your team different from other teams?
- What might you offer in terms of expertise, support, or shared projects?
- How can your team benefit from interacting with other teams?
- What is in it for you? For the other team?

CONTACT WITH OTHER TEAMS

Identify the contact person

Identify the major focus and tasks

Determine how your team can work together with other teams to "leverage" your efforts

Determine what information can help your team

SET UP PROCEDURES FOR WORKING WITH OTHER TEAMS

Determine the objective(s) for working with another team

Find out which teams you will work with

Who will represent your team?

What is the team representative expected to do?

How long will the team representative have the position?

BALANCING TASK AND PEOPLE FOCUS

As in any work environment, the AQP team is always trying to find a balance between the tasks that are required for completion of the project and the people affected. Unless a balance between tasks (results) and relationships (people) is recognized, the team may not act effectively and the desired end results may prove to be elusive. Therefore, to enhance team effectiveness and the efficiency of the team process, appropriate roles for everyone must be established and all expectations must be defined up front. Some guidelines to help the team towards this goal are:

A team can focus on tasks, people, or reaching a balance between the two. When focusing on tasks, the emphasis is on what the team does to accomplish the task, actions that help the team reach its goal, accomplish an immediate task, make a decision, or solve a problem, and content and results. Being task-oriented includes ensuring that the purpose is fully understood, clarifying jargon used, identifying owners, clarifying expectations, identifying related issues (both supports and obstacles), and visualizing and anticipating results.

When focusing on people, the emphasis is on how the team goes about accomplishing its task, using team relationships to more efficiently and effectively accomplish its goals, and process and relationships. Being people-oriented includes encouraging buy-in, motivating members by encouraging change through their contributions to the team, addressing members' concerns and expectations, looking for similarities among members to aid in achieving a cohesive team, relating individual tasks to expertise and ability, and encouraging responsibility and accountability.

When reaching a balance between tasks and people, the emphasis is on balance, however, there is no magic combination. It all depends on the project.

Facilitating Skills

As we already have mentioned, an effective team demands a capable facilitator. However, the facilitator's skill is the engine that will propel the AQP team towards the completion of the project assignment. Some of the techniques and some typical examples are shown in Table 5.

Table 5. Techniques and Examples Used by an Effective Facilitator

Technique	Examples
Clarify assignments	Align individual assignments with team objectives Agree on deadlines Clarify any questions and ask for feedback Make changes based on feedback
Distribute assignments fairly	Consider team member's abilities, expertise, and access to information Ask for volunteers Consider team member's workload
Create a supportive environment	Help prioritize the tasks and steps of a task Encourage members to share assignments Encourage each member to contribute Be realistic about deadlines, recognizing responsibilities outside the team
Document assignments	Document meeting minutes and/or action plans that identify team assignments, responsibilities, and completion dates Distribute minutes to all members Encourage pre-planning to save time with discussions and making decisions
Ask members to distribute report(s) prior to the team meeting	Discussion and decision-making

REFERENCE

Allen, R.W. and Porter, L.W. (Eds). *Organizational Influence Processes*. Glenview, IL: Scott, Freeman, 1983.

Eienburg, E.M. and Witten, M.G. "Reconsidering Openess in Organizational Communication." *Academy of Management Review* Vol. 12 (1987): 418-426.

Moran, L., Musselwhite, E. and Zenger, J.H. *Keeping Teams on Track*. Burr Ridge, IL: Irwin Professional, 1996.

Robbins, S.P. *Managing Organizational Conflict*. Englewood Cliffs, NJ: Prentice Hall, 1974.

Roming, D.A. *Breakthrough Teamwork*. Burr Ridge, IL: Irwin Professional, 1996.

Sholtes, P.R. *The Team Handbook*. Madison, WI: Joiner Associates, 1989.

FOUR

Scheduling

Crucial to the development of AQP is the proper timing, tracking, and implementation of each product/process planning step. The proper timing for the execution of the quality disciplines is critical to the success of the AQP program. A documented critical path timing or schedule-timing plan is essential.

To introduce a product/process that is on-time, meets the customer's quality needs, and is within budget, critical path timing or schedule-timing must be used. When an organization properly manages the schedule-timing element of AQP, it can achieve significant improvements in development costs, manufacturing costs, and on-time launching of products, and lessen the need to "put out fires" while launching a new product/process. Furthermore, design changes in product/processes that result in tooling changes that drive costs up can be reduced and/or more prudently handled. The AQP team, based on their experience, knowledge, and intuition, can, with a disciplined timing program approach, evaluate their alternatives and proceed to make more effective, informed decisions.

CHOOSE OR DEVELOP A METHOD FOR TRACKING YOUR PROGRESS

To facilitate critical path timing or schedule-timing, it is strongly recommended that a carefully chosen and developed method be established for tracking progress toward objectives. A system should be devised that addresses the need to handle the inevitable disruptions and changes in product/process planning and manufacturing. To be workable, timing plans must incorporate and recognize the capacity constraints of staff availability. Otherwise, inevitable disruptions of product/process changes will occur.

Charts

There are many charts to use, depending on the objective of the project and the outcome desired. For example, process flow charts, check-off sheets, and outlines of the elements and scheduling components of an AQP program provide a comprehensive list of the tasks, concerns, assignments, and other events that the AQP team directs from the inception of the program through final sign-off. Status reports are to be prepared from the charts using "start" and "completion" dates and actual points of progress. Using the charts, the team identifies items that need attention. Computer software packages which generate Gantt (milestone chart) or critical path charts are an acceptable choice. The advantages will be discussed in the next section.

An example of this charting is the concept to customer (CTC) process flow chart, which is an integral part of the Ford AQP schedule-timing concept. This is particularly useful for Ford supplier guidance. This process establishes timing points (also known as diamond points) that Ford expects to be met within 30 months during a new model vehicle launch. A quality planning team for a Ford supplier must assure that the timing plans for the product/process support the CTC concept.

Planning teams should be aware of need for supplier input on design and process developments for products designed by the supplier (sometimes referred to as black or gray box parts) or by the specific customer.

Computer Software Programs

For the management and assessment of all the aspects and the repercussions related to establishing critical path timing or schedule timing, a computer schedule or project management program can be the best answer. (There are many commercial software programs available, however, it seems that the automotive industry is using primarily Harvard Project Management and Microsoft Project.) A project management or schedule-timing software product can track all elements of the AQP program. The team is better able to analyze options quickly, often in seconds or minutes. Using quantified options, they are able to control product/process inventories and make correct, informed decisions for schedule-timing. When they are able to critically analyze options quickly and easily, they are less apt to choose the most obvious answer that often is just a band-aid approach to solving AQP options. Performing careful *needs analysis* is advised before purchasing any new software products incorporating the following constraints: staff availability, materials inventories, and production capability. Remember, a correctly chosen computer software program allows you to make prompt, competent timing, and schedule changes that can be printed quickly and then distributed to the team and management for action.

Critical path timing or schedule-timing programs provide the added advantage of gaining time for more prudent resource use. Ultimately, improved schedule timing introduces the ability to react to changes with facts quickly. Improved response time to problem solving in emergency situations leads to cost reductions. All of these factors, in turn, allow schedulers even more opportunity for improving the AQP planning production/process.

In addition, if a fully integrated computer integrated manufacturing (CIM) schedule-timing system is provided, important added benefits are available to the AQP team for communicating to management the implications of costs and savings. For instance, graphical presentations allow others to understand easily the impact of various schedule-timing options. Ultimately, proper critical path timing or schedule-timing provides even more opportunity to improve product/processes, which ensures continual as well as cycle time improvement.

Obviously, for each individual organization and product orientation there is a planning check-off list. In addition, individual customers may have their own reporting mechanisms, so that they keep track of the supplier progress. A typical quality planning check-off list is shown in Table 6. Tables 7-9 identify the requirements for Chrysler, Ford, and General Motors.

Table 6. Typical Quality Planning Check-Off List

Quality Systems
    Is the system approved by the customer?
    Prints/specifications
    Design FMEA/failure product analysis (FPA)

Key Characteristics
    Are design actions identified?
    Can product be manufactured, assembled, and tested?
    Are preventive process actions identified?
    Field/plant concerns
    Are engineering changes required?

Feasibility Analysis
    Have customer requirements been identified and taken into consideration?
    Process/inspection flow chart
    Process FMEA
    Equipment
    Previous statistical studies (surrogate data may be used)
    Design of experiments
    Cause and effect diagram
    Have characteristics for sensitive processes been identified for SPC?
    Can control charts be used on all key characteristics?
    Can causes of field/plant concerns be monitored?

Manufacturing Analysis
    Quality systems/procedures
    Key product/process characteristics
    Sample size/frequency
    Inspection methods
    Reaction plan
    Statistical methods
    Problem-solving discipline
    Are operating and SPC procedures sufficient to make control plan work?
    Is 100% inspection required?
    Does the control plan have customer concurrence?

Process Potential Study
    Statistical training
    Implementation
    Results
      Is the process ready for sign-off?
      Are process changes needed to improve feasibility?

Process Sign-Off
    Process sheets
    Inspection instructions
    Test equipment/gage
    Initial samples
    Packaging
      Was the process FMEA used to develop process sheets?
      Was the process FMEA used to develop a dynamic control plan?
      Does customer feedback suggest control plan changes?
      Does the process conform to control plan requirements?

Table 7. Chrysler's Advanced Quality Planning Schedule

Feasibility sign-off
Major characteristics
Field failure mode analysis
Consuming plant concerns
Design FMEA (tooling)
Gage design
Previous statistical studies
Process FMEA
Prototype parts
Process flow diagram
Factory floor plan
New equipment list
Manufacturing control plan
Process potential studies
Process sign-off
Process sheet
Initial samples
Packaging design

Table 8. Ford's Advanced Quality Planning Status Reporting

Sourcing decisions
    Alternative suppliers
    Customer awareness
Customer input requirements
Design FMEA
Design reviews
Design verification plan
Subcontractor APQP status
Facilities, tools, and gages
Prototype build control plan
Prototype builds
Drawing and specifications
Team feasibility commitment
Manufacturing process flow chart
Process FMEA
Measurement systems evaluation
Pre-launch control plan
Operator process instructions
Packaging specifications
Production trial run
Production control plan
Preliminary process capability study
Production validation testing
Production part approval (PSW)
Part submission warrant (PSW) part delivery at material required date (MRD)

Table 9. General Motor's Advanced Quality Planning Status Reporting

Design FMEA
Design reviews
Design verification plan
Facilities, tools, and gages
Prototype build control plan
Prototype builds
Drawing and specifications
Team feasibility commitment
Manufacturing process flow chart
Process FMEA
Measurement systems evaluation
Pre-launch control plan
Operator process instructions
Packaging specifications
Production trial run
Production control plan
Preliminary process capability study
Production validation testing
Production part approval (PPA)

WORK BREAKDOWN STRUCTURES (WBS)

A WBS is a hierarchical format that organizes and divides the project into manageable units. To optimize the planning and scheduling timing of the advanced quality planning project, an appropriate understanding of WBS is essential. In this section we will summarize the key aspects of WBS.

The critical component of WBS development is scope development. Scope development is the process of creating a written scope statement as the basis for future project decisions, including the criteria used to determine if the project has been completed successfully. An example of a scope statement includes:

organizational information such as the

    project name,

    champion, and

    team members;

project information such as

    description and deliverables,

purpose,

assumptions,

project benefits, and

completion criteria including measurement method;

timing objectives such as

expected target start date,

expected project completion date, and

project milestones;

coordination issues such as

product equipment release,

outside support,

special equipment and

special issues,

(procurement), and;

safety and environmental issues like

governmental requirements,

local requirements, and

job requirements.

Once the scope has been defined, then the WBS is developed. A WBS is a hierarchical format that organizes and divides total scope of the project into manageable units. Each descending level of any WBS is represented by an increasingly detailed description. An example of a WBS structure is shown in Figure 5.

Specifically, a WBS is used to

develop or confirm common understanding of project scope,

identify project deliverables,

initiate planning process,

control and track the project,

identify work packages and assign responsibilities,

communicate project strategy, and

assist in reporting.

Figure 5—An example of a work breakdown structure (WBS).

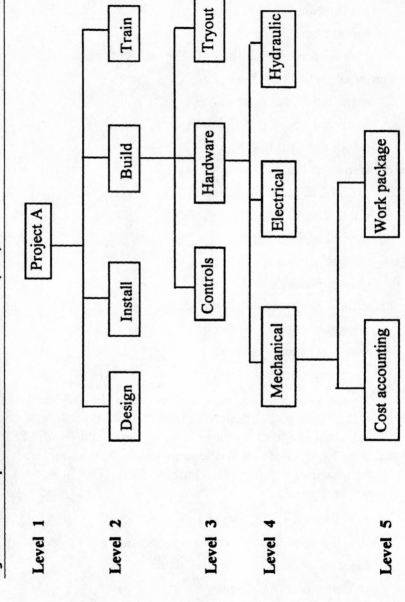

Level 1

Level 2

Level 3

Level 4

Level 5

WBS DEVELOPMENT PROCESS

Because of WBS's importance in any scheduling endeavor, we summarize the process of development steps:

1. Identify major elements of the project. In general, the major elements will be the project deliverables. Sometimes, different criteria can be used to determine major elements:

   Phases of project life cycle can be used as the first level of decomposition, with project deliverables listed at the second level; or

   the organizing principle of the WBS may vary. Organizational structure, bill of material, or reporting requirements may define WBS formats.

2. Decide if an adequate resource and duration estimate can be developed at this level of detail for each element. The meaning of adequate may change over the course of the project. Further decomposition may not be possible for an element that will be accomplished far in the future. For each element, proceed to step 4 if there is adequate detail and to step 3 if there is not.

3. Continue the decomposition process to identify sub-elements for each element requiring further decomposition and repeat step 2.

4. Verify the correctness of WBS by asking the following questions:

   Are the lower level items both necessary and sufficient?

   Can each item be clearly and completely defined?

   Can each item be appropriately scheduled, budgeted, and assigned to an organizational unit, team, or person?

Activity Definition

Activity definition involves identifying and documenting activities to produce work package deliverables identified in WBS. Activities can be defined in various ways. The commonly used method is the continuation of the decomposition process initiated in WBS development. This process usually applies to unique, first-time projects. Decomposition of WBS continues until the lowest level elements, which are activities, are reached. An activity must meet the following criteria. It must:

- Have a tangible objective (deliverable).

- Be measurable.

- Have an expected duration. The length of the duration must not be too long or too short. The rule of thumb is that the activity duration should not exceed the length of the reporting period. If there are weekly progress meetings, then the duration of the activity should be 1 week or less.

- Have an expected resource requirements and cost.

- Include procedural steps, sometimes referred to as tasks. For example, every phase of the AQP includes certain deliverables and within these deliverables several individual tasks are required for proper completion. The task (activity) includes a detailed procedure to ensure quality completion.

  Other methods can be used to define activities for repetitive or similar projects.

  As in AQP project management, templates can be used to define activities. In addition, previous projects can be utilized to expedite the activity development process.

Activity vs. Task

The words "task" and "activity" are used interchangeably in this book and elsewhere. In AQP project management, tasks and activities are identical. However, tasks also often are referred to as procedural steps of an activity.

Activity Sequencing

Activities must be sequenced to support development of a realistic and achievable schedule. The output of this process is a project network logic diagram (NLD). NLD is a schematic display of the project's activities and logical relationships among them. The following information must be available to start the sequencing of activities:

ACTIVITY LIST. Activity list is the product of the activity definition process.

MANDATORY DEPENDENCIES. Mandatory dependencies are those inherent in the nature of the work being done. For example, you cannot install the press crown before erecting the uprights. Mandatory dependencies are also called "hard logic."

DISCRETIONARY DEPENDENCIES. Discretionary dependencies are those defined by the project planning team based on experience, best practices, historical information, and other considerations. Discretionary dependencies are also called "preferred legion" or "soft logic." For example, installing Press 2 loader before Press 1 loader.

EXTERNAL DEPENDENCIES. External dependencies are those that involve a relationship between project activities and nonproject activities. For example, a die construction and tryout project is dependent on the release of engineering information.

CONSTRAINTS. Constraints are factors that limit the project scheduling options. They are predetermined project milestones. For example, TTO must happen 5.5 months before Job 1 and all preceding activities must be scheduled to ensure that it happens.

TYPES OF ACTIVITY RELATIONSHIPS

There are four types of relationships:

1. Finish-to-Start (FS). The "from" activity must finish before the "to" activity can start. For example, first die tryout cannot start until the dies are delivered.

2. Finish-to-Finish (FF). The "from" activity must finish before the "to" activity can finish. For example, the quality tasks during first die tryout cannot be finished before the tryout is finished.

3. Start-to-Start (SS): The "from" activity must start before the "to" activity. For example, quality tasks can be started some time after the first die tryout starts. In other words, we don't have to wait until the first die tryout is complete to start the quality actions.

4. Start-to-Finish (SF): The "from" activity must start before the "to" activity can finish. For example: collecting the data must be started before the report is written. FS is the most commonly used type of relationship. SF relationship is rarely used. FF and SS relationships allow the overlapping of activities.

LAG TIME

Usually, SS and FF relationships are defined with a time delay, which determines the amount of overlap allowed. Lag time on an FS relationship creates a delay for the start of the "to" activity. For example:

- The quality tasks can start only after the certain number of panels are produced during the first die set, and this may take one day. Therefore, we would define the relationship between first die set and quality activities as SS 1d (Start-to-Start with 1 day lag time).

- During a press installation, the relationship between erecting the crown and wiring the crown can be defined as FF 2d. The wiring of the crown can start before the erecting of the crown is finished but cannot be completed until 2 days after the erecting of the crown.

- In a construction project, the relationship between pouring cement and removing forms can be represented as FS 21d. The 21-day lag time will allow the concrete to set.

SCHEDULE DEVELOPMENT

Schedule development means determining start and finish dates for project activities. There are three mathematical techniques to calculate start and finish dates:

1. Critical Path Method (CPM): CPM calculates a single, deterministic early and late start and finish date for each activity based on specified, sequential network logic and single duration estimate.

2. Program Evaluation and Review Technique (PERT): PERT uses sequential network logic and probabilistic duration estimates to calculate activity dates. PERT produces three sets of dates (optimistic, most likely, pessimistic) for early and late start and finish dates.

3. Graphical Evaluation and Review Technique (GERT): GERT allows probabilistic treatment of both network logic and duration estimate in calculating activity dates.

Critical Path Methodology (CPM)

Most frequently, CPM is used to calculate the start and finish dates. The CPM algorithm is performed in four steps:

1) establish project calendar,

2) forward pass,

3) backward pass, and

4) critical path analysis.

ESTABLISHING THE PROJECT CALENDAR

Project calendars identify periods when work is allowed. Specifically, they:

Indicate the amount of time available for work (e.g., number of shifts per day, number of hours per shift) and

indicate the non-work times (i.e., holidays, vacations, weekends, etc.).

Projects may have multiple calendars. For example, suppliers may be allowed to perform their activities only during the weekdays while the plant personnel can work during the weekends also. In this case, two calendars would be created: a 7 day/week calendar for the plant personnel activities and a 5 day/week calendar for the vendor activities.

Forward Pass

In this step, the early start and finish dates and overall project duration are calculated.

1. Early start (ES). Earliest date an activity can start.
2. Early finish (EF): Earliest date an activity can finish.
3. Overall project duration: The duration of the longest path.

Forward Pass is performed as follows:

1. For the first activity (activity with no predecessor) calculate

   ES = project start date;

   EF = ES + duration − 1.

   If there are multiple activities with no predecessors, they will all have the same ES.

2. Move forward to the right to the next activity and calculate:

   ES = latest EF of preceding activities + 1;

   EF = ES + duration − 1.

3. Repeat 2 until all activities are covered.
4. Calculate:

   Project end date = Latest EF of activities with no successor;

   overall project duration = project end date − project start date + 1.

Backward Pass

This step calculates the late start and finish dates.

   LS: Latest date an activity can start;

   LF: Latest date an activity can finish.

Backward Pass is performed as follows:

1. Starting from the last activity (activity with no successor), calculate:

   LF = project end date;

   LS = LF − duration + 1.

If there are multiple activities with no successors, they will all have the same LF.

Occasionally, projects have predetermined finish dates (finish constraint, Job 1, etc.). In this case, regardless of calculated project end date, LF for the last activity is set equal to the predetermined finish date.

2. Move backward to the left to the previous activity:

LF = earliest LF of Succeeding Activities − 1;

LS = LF − duration +1.

3. Repeat 2 until all activities are covered.

Critical Path Analysis (CP)

Once all early and late start and finish dates are calculated, CP analysis can be conducted to determine the critical path and identify critical activities. To determine the critical path, we must first calculate activity total float (slack) times. Total float (TF) for an activity is defined as the amount of time the activity can be delayed without delaying the project end date. It is the time between the LF and EF dates.

TF = LF − EF

Critical Path is defined as the longest path in the network logic diagram. Activities in the critical path are critical activities and they must be monitored closely. Critical paths may change throughout the project life-cycle based on progress. The project management team must be careful to identify critical activities after each update period. Specifically, the determination of a CP is to:

• Calculate TF for each activity

• Identify and connect activities with zero or negative total float. The path revealed is the critical path. There may be multiple critical paths, depending on the chosen characteristic (for example: time, manpower, cost, and so on).

For a simple example, see the figure of how to construct a house. Note the dark line indicating the critical path.

Table 10. Sample of Schedule Statistics and Critical Path Information for the House Construction Project

Sequence	Activity	Activity Time (days)	Start Early	Start Late	Finish Early	Finish Late	Slack
1-2	start	0	0	3	0	3	3
2-3	excavate and pour footings	4	0	3	4	7	3
3-4	pour concrete foundation	2	4	7	6	9	3
4-5	erect frame including rough roof	4	6	9	10	13	3
5-6	lay brickwork	6	10	21	16	27	11
4-7	install basement drains and plumbing	1	6	10	7	11	4
7-8	pour basement floor	2	7	11	9	13	4
7-9	install rough plumbing	3	7	14	10	17	7
5-9	install rough wiring	2	10	15	12	17	5
8-9	install heating and ventilating	4	10	13	14	17	3
9-10	fasten plaster board and plaster, including drying	10	14	17	24	27	3
10-11	laying finish flooring	3	24	27	27	30	3
11-12	install kitchen fixtures	1	27	31	28	32	4
11-13	install finish plumbing	2	27	30	29	32	3
11-17	finish carpentry	3	27	32	30	35	5
6-15	finish roofing and flashing	2	16	27	18	29	11
15-16	fasten gutters and downspouts	1	18	29	19	30	11
4-16	lay storm drains for rain water	1	6	29	7	30	23
17-19	sand and varnish flooring	2	32	35	34	37	3
13-14	paint	3	29	32	32	35	3
14-19	finish electrical work	1	32	36	33	37	4
16-18	finish grading	2	19	30	21	32	11
18-19	pour walks and complete landscaping	5	21	32	26	37	11
19-20	finish	0	34	37	34	37	3
5-8	dummy	0	10	13	10	13	3
12-13	dummy	0	28	32	28	32	4
14-17	dummy	0	32	35	32	35	3

RESOURCE PLANNING

Since the entire AQP is planning, it stands to reason that one of the major components of scheduling is the resource planning activities. Resource planning involves determining what physical resources (people, equipment, materials) and what quantities of each are required to conduct project activities.

Figure 6—PERT network diagram for a house construction project. The dark line indicates the critical path.

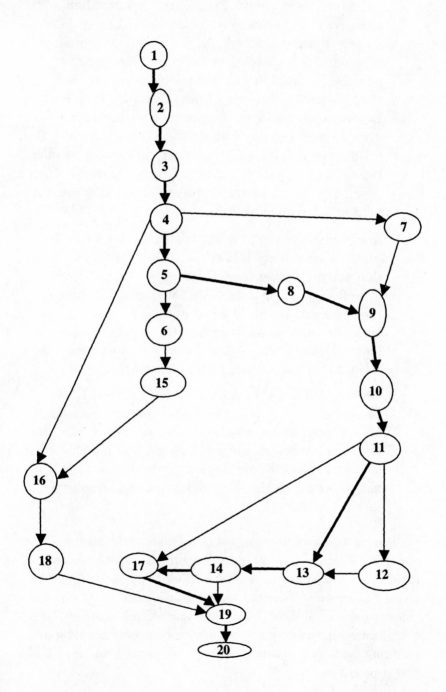

Resource planning is performed in three steps: .

1. Define resource library. Frequently, resource limitations are the main reasons for missed schedule dates. To create realistic schedules, the planning team must consider the availability of resources. Resource libraries are used to define available resources and their quantities throughout the project life-cycle. Resource calendars are also used to further define availabilities. For example, a project's calendar may be a 7 day/week, 8 hour/day calendar; however, a specific resource may be available only 5 days a week. In this case, activities requiring this specific resource will not be scheduled on weekends.

2. Assign resources to project activities: Duration estimate for an activity is based on resources allocated to that activity. For example, if it takes 10 days to perform floor work on a set of dies with two die makers, the same activity could be completed in only 5 days with four die makers. However, this is just an example and in reality changes in resource allocations may not affect activity durations proportionately.

3. Perform "what-ifs" to determine optimum schedule (baseline): This step involves performing various trade-off scenarios to establish optimum schedules using the resource leveling technique. Resource leveling modifies schedules based on resource availabilities. Frequently, activity schedule dates are delayed due to resource unavailability.

During resource leveling, activities are delayed based on activity priorities, which are determined by the planning team. Also, the planning, team may change activity sequences, modify calendars, increase resource availability, or use outside resources to offset delays and scheduling problems. The optimization process requires interaction between resource planning, activity definition, activity sequencing, and cost budgeting processes.

COST BUDGETING

Cost budgeting involves allocating the overall cost estimates to individual work items in order to establish a cost baseline for measuring project performance. Cost budgeting is dependent on the resource planning process. Activity costs may include:

resource cost = amount of resource x unit cost,

other fixed costs, or

both.

In AQP, the financial model that is used to calculate specific activities and projects is either the standard cost or activity-based costing. Each AQP task is assigned resources which in turn are used to estimate the cost of that task.

PROJECT PLAN DEVELOPMENT

Project plan development uses the outputs of the other planning processes to create a consistent, coherent document that can be used to guide both project execution and project control. This is an iterative process. For example, the initial plan may include generic resources and durations while the final plan reflects specific resources and explicit dates. Project plans can be very complex depending on project requirements. They may include:

- Baseline project schedule
- Project assumptions
- Project constraints
- Risk plan which identifies potential risks and includes action plans to avoid or mitigate identified risks
- Communication plan including types of reports and a distribution plan
- Quality plan
- Change control plan
- AQP team training

Perhaps two of the newest and most promising techniques that are being introduced in the United States are TRIZ and the structured inventive thinking (SIT) methodologies.

THEORY OF INVENTIVE PROBLEM SOLVING (TRIZ)

The goal of TRIZ and SIT is to reduce the generation time and improve the quality of innovative solutions to technical problems by providing a structure for developing solutions, including the systematical accessing of prior innovation across industry.

The innovation methodologies TRIZ and SIT are used to structure a problem and generate solution concepts. TRIZ is a Russian acronym for Theory of Inventive Problem Solving and is the result of over 50 years of research and development that began in the former Soviet Union. Through this research, it was recognized that the same fundamental problem or contradiction had often been addressed by a number of inventions, but in different areas of technology. In addition, it was discovered that the same fundamental inventive principles and subsequent solutions were used over and over again, often separated by many years. The research scientists sought to extract, compile, and organize this knowledge and reasoned that if later inventors had had knowledge of the earlier solutions, their task would have been straightforward.

TRIZ methodically examines inventive problems, exploring the entire solution space and developing conceptual solutions. It is a means for reaching across engineering disciplines to solve problems by using solutions from various areas of technology and industry. TRIZ generalizes worldwide experience in invention, systematizes successful methods of solving technological problems, and reveals regularities in the evolution of technological systems. This methodology is gaining popularity in the industrial community as companies expand their engineering competency from a corporate "lessons learned" knowledge base to a cross-industry technology base.

The TRIZ process follows four phases. They are:

(PHASE 1) BACKGROUND INFORMATION. We begin this phase by working closely with the subject matter experts (SMEs) to review any prior test data/methods and prior solution attempts to learn from past experience and ensure that there will be no duplication of effort. In addition, informal interviews and a review of the manufacturing processes are conducted with available SMEs to acquire additional information that may not have been documented. In parallel with the above, we collect benchmarking information and conduct a patent search to establish the state of the art.

(PHASE 2) PROBLEM FORMULATION. At this point, we develop a technical description of the problem and define the contradiction(s) that prevent a straightforward solution. It is imperative that the team members adopt a structured thought process that breaks psychological inertia and reduces the "not-invented-here" syndrome at this point in the process. It is of paramount importance that all participants who are to use the TRIZ methodology be familiar with the thought process of the methodology.

(PHASE 3) SOLUTION DEVELOPMENT. By this time in the project, the problem has been properly described and the contradiction(s) defined; this typically results in the development of a fair number of conceptual solutions. To ensure coverage of the entire solution space, the team then works with the TRIZ software. This allows the team to look across engineering disciplines and identify potential solutions to the problem that may have been applied in other industries. In addition, the team formally documents each solution concept, prepares invention disclosures, begins a preliminary feasibility study, and develops a verification testing recommendation.

(PHASES 4 AND 5) FEASIBILITY AND DESIGN VERIFICATION. Appropriate feasibility and reliability techniques are applied to ensure that each design concept is robust.

PRIMARY ADVANTAGE. Both TRIZ and SIT methodologies focus the solution efforts on the technical root cause(s) of the problem and provide systematic, disciplined ways to translate a general problem into a specific technical objective that can be solved by using the general inventive principles contained within these methodologies. These principles are drawn from many diverse engineering disciplines and provide engineers with solutions that are often outside their areas of expertise.

PRIMARY DISADVANTAGE. This process requires a TRIZ expert to effectively utilize the TRIZ computer tools, structure the problem, and develop a problem prioritization strategy. There are currently very few qualified TRIZ experts in the U.S., however, as more people become proficient with the TRIZ methodology (in 3 to 5 years), there will be no limit to the number of problems that can be addressed using this technique.

STRUCTURED INVENTIVE THINKING (SIT)

Structured Inventive Thinking (SIT) is an extension of TRIZ, conceived in Israel by TRIZ practitioners with the goal of making the TRIZ methodology more accessible and easier to learn. By employing a structured approach to problem solving, it helps to focus the problem solver on the essence of the problem, to overcome psychological barriers to creative thinking, and to enable the discovery of inventive solutions.

The SIT methodology deals with conceptual solutions to technological problems. Its purpose is to focus the problem solver on the essence of the problem, to overcome psychological barriers to creative thinking, to enable the discovery of inventive solutions, and to make the process efficient. It does this by guiding the user through either of two algorithms (see Fig. 7), which structure the problem in such a way as to allow the user to apply various techniques that help to inspire creative solutions. SIT deals with the pre-engineering phase of problem solving, which enables the identification of alternative solutions to problems. It does not replace conventional problem-solving methodologies, but rather it supplements these by giving the engineer/scientist another problem solving tool—one that emphasizes invention, the product of creativity.

Figure 7—The structured inventive thinking (SIT) model.

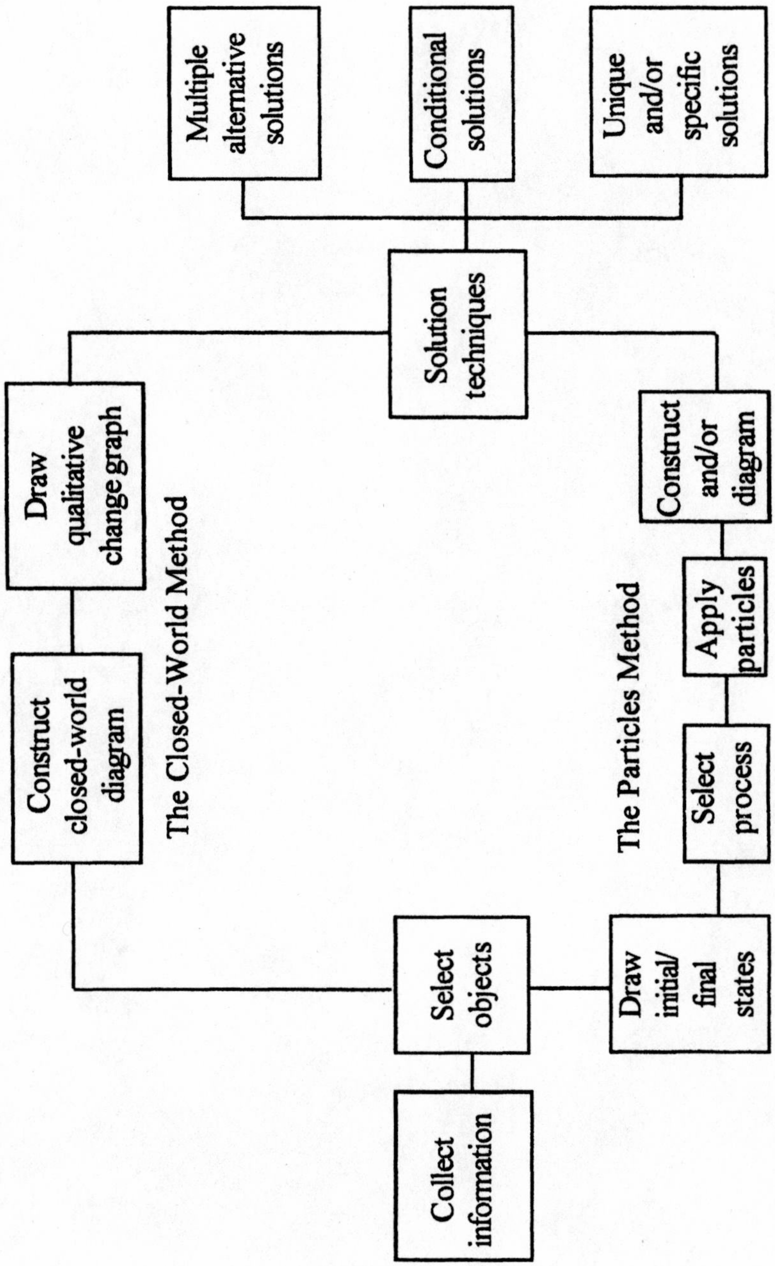

FIVE

Create a Product Definition

Product definition is a comprehensive and critical review of engineering requirements and other required elements of the design product/process. Listings of significant or critical product/process characteristics are developed, feasibility is analyzed, and drawings and material specifications are produced. Appropriate techniques that might be instituted during this phase of product/process definition are design of experiments, design for manufacturing, design for assembly, and many others.

DETERMINING FEASIBILITY

Feasibility analysis is an evaluation which is based on a series of assessments. The objective is to determine if a design can be manufactured, assembled, tested, packed, and transported while maintaining acceptable quality standards.

For a design to be proven "feasible" it must be capable of facilitating planned production volumes and schedules. The design must meet engineering requirements, quality and reliability criteria, unit cost objectives, and desired timing.

In addition, because of globalization, at this stage it is also important to be familiar with the customs regulations of the country of origin or transport. Different countries require quite different paper trails for transport, and, as a consequence, delays may be encountered, causing deliveries to be late.

Feasibility analysis is required from design conception through engineering release.

DESIGN FMEA AND DESIGN FEASIBILITY

The design FMEA, as a technique for identifying potential problems, is essential to determining design feasibility. Without the identification of probable problems and an early capability assessment of high risk priority items, product/process control is unlikely. Table 11 displays a typical sample of a feasibility information checklist for a design FMEA.

Table 11. A Typical Feasibility Information Checklist for a Design FMEA

Comment and or Condition	YES or NO	Action Required
Does the design FMEA identify operations that effect "high risk priority" failure modes?		
Have previous manufacturing experiences indicated that "high risk priority" operations are not capable?		
Will "high risk priority" operations utilize new or untried processes?		
Have operations for statistical capability studies been identified?		
Will a process FMEA be conducted?		
Should major casual factors be analyzed using a design of experiments?		
Have all customs regulations (if applicable) been reviewed?		

DESIGN (FMEA) AS A QUALITY TOOL

The design FMEA is a problem-solving tool used to prevent potential problems or correct product/process design failures prior to release of the print. It is used to assure that quality is designed into the product/process and not inspected into the product/process later. Failure to perform the design FMEA results in existing problem(s) reappearing in future products and an increased likelihood that customer needs and various regulatory requirements from government agencies will not be met.

The design FMEA is a "living document" for determining the probability of the occurrence of a failure and the severity of the effect of that failure if it occurs. The design FMEA formalizes the engineer's thought processes. It is, in effect, a summary analysis of every item that could go wrong based on prior experience and past problems. For that reason, the design FMEA is to be created early in the critical path of the design or schedule-timing of AQP. By addressing the issues of design failures early, the chances are decreased that extra cost expenditures and/or delayed product/process project release dates will occur. The AQP team is to consider a design FMEA as component of the initial quality assessment phase of product design. Provisions are also to be made for updates that reflect the latest actions and design levels. To expedite submission and maintenance of FMEA documents, proper training and the use of computer software products are recommended.

During the design FMEA portion of AQP, the selection of significant and control or key characteristics is accomplished. The selected significant and control or key characteristics are to be noted on a product's specifications, prints, design verification tests, and wherever else applicable. Suppliers providing product/process design, e.g., black box or gray box product, are responsible for submitting a design FMEA. An example of the design FMEA form is shown in Figure 8. For a detailed discussion of FMEA, see Stamatis (1995).

DEVELOPING DRAWING AND MATERIAL SPECIFICATIONS

Control plans for engineering drawings include and show any critical government, safety, and regulatory characteristics. If customer engineering drawings are not available, the supplier is to review which dimensions affect fit, function, and durabil-

Figure 8—A typical design FMEA form.

System _____
Subsystem _____
Component _____
Model _____

Design responsibility _____
Due Date _____
Core Team _____

FMEA Number _____
Page ___ of ___
Prepared By _____
FMEA date (Orig.) _____ Rev. _____

Item/ Function	Potential Failure Mode	Potential Effect(s) of Failure	S E V	C R I T	Potential Cause(s) Mechanism(s) of Failure	O C C U R	Current Design Controls	D E T E C	R P N	Recommended Action(s)	Responsibility and Target Completion Date	ACTION RESULTS				
												Action Taken	S E V	O C C	D E T	R P N

ity plus any government, safety, and regulatory requirements as described in the engineering specification, previous warranty experience, or assembly drawings.

Drawing reviews should be conducted to determine if there are sufficient dimensions for part set-up and to minimize inspection error. Datum and control lines should be defined for appropriate development of control gages. Accepted manufacturing standards should be defined for process measurements. Functional and durability requirements of components and assemblies are to be determined and listed in control plans. Check engineering specifications for sample size, frequency, and acceptance criteria. In all cases, the supplier should determine characteristics that affect or control the functional and durability requirements.

Material specifications should be reviewed for significant or critical characteristics relating to properties, performance, environmental, handling, and storage requirements. These characteristics should be included in the control plan.

SIGNIFICANT OR CRITICAL CHARACTERISTICS

Special controls are necessary for significant or critical characteristics. Key or major significant or critical characteristics must be identified on the control plan. Significant or critical characteristics are to be identified by suppliers, as well as by customers, especially if these characteristics have legal or safety implications. As the design and feasibility review is conducted, other significant or critical characteristics are identified in an ongoing systematic analysis.

Suitable characteristics are identified using the following variability factors that need special controls:

- Design FMEAs

- Process FMEAs

- Performance specifications

- Cause and effect diagrams

A typical sample of a feasibility information checklist for significant characteristics is shown in Table 12.

Table 12. A Typical Feasibility Information Checklist for Significant Characteristics

Comment and or Conditions	YES or NO	Action Required
Have characteristics been identified that ensure performance specifications will be met?		
Have historical customer concerns been identified?		
Have characteristics been identified that affect fit, function, durability, and conformance to government regulations?		
Were key characteristics identified using a cause and effect diagram or any other tool of equal or greater value?		
Were critical characteristics identified using the design and process FMEA?		

ENGINEERING DRAWINGS AND DESIGN FEASIBILITY

- Drawings must be evaluated and reviewed to establish if there is adequate dimensional information available on the individual part to facilitate setup and minimize inspection error.

- Control (datum) lines should be called out so that design can be initiated for functional gages to effect ongoing controls. (This applies only in the case of GT & D drawings.)

- Process dimensions should be reviewed and evaluated to establish if they are "containable" and consistent with accepted standards for manufacturing.

- Engineering drawings should include critical and/or key characteristics that must be identified on the control plan. If none are present, as in the case of proprietary designs, the customer must be consulted for review of the design to determine which dimensions affect fit, function, durability, and government regulations.

A typical feasibility information checklist for engineering drawings is shown in Table 13.

Table 13. A Typical Feasibility Information Checklist for Engineering Drawings

Comment and or Conditions	YES or NO	Action Required
Have you identified how the dimensions affect fit, durability, and function?		
Have you identified sufficient dimensions to minimize inspection layout time?		
Can you design functional gages? Have sufficient datum lines and control points been identified?		
Have tolerances been assessed to be compatible with manufacturing standards?		
Can tolerance stackups be contained?		
Can all requirements specified be evaluated using known inspection techniques?		
Have features dimensions been checked to eliminate loss of tolerance during normal processing?		

ENGINEERING SPECIFICATIONS AND DESIGN FEASIBILITY

- Assure that function and durability specifications are met by determining which characteristics in the part design affect or control results.

- Review the "controlling specification" in an effort to assess the functional and durability requirements of the component or assembly.

- Consult the engineering specification to determine if the sample size, frequency, and acceptance criteria are in some instances set forth in the "in-process test section." If this is not the case, sample size and frequency must be determined and called out in the control plan. The control plan must be reviewed and approved by the customer.

A typical feasibility information checklist for engineering specifications (ES) is shown in Table 14.

Table 14. A Typical Feasibility Information Checklist for Engineering Specifications (ES)

Comment and or Conditions	YES or NO	Action Required
Is test loading sufficient to provide conditions, i.e., production validation, ongoing and annual certification?		
Can regularly scheduled in-process tests be conducted if the action plan requires additional samples to be tested?		
Will any portion of the ES testing be done outside?		
Has identification been made of dimensional or material characteristics that effect ES results for inclusion in the control plan?		
Are all specified tests and acceptance criteria clearly defined and understood?		
Are materials compatible with the coefficient for variation (e.g., for expansion/contraction) with regard to specification and/or equipment?		

MATERIALS SPECIFICATIONS AND DESIGN FEASIBILITY

Review materials specifications for occurrences of significant and critical characteristics relating to

> performance, environmental, handling, and warehouse requirements, properties, and

> identifying significant and critical characteristics as they relate to materials specifications on the control plan.

Using the materials specifications, use the checklist to review the product/process.

A typical feasibility information checklist for materials specification is shown in Table 15.

Table 15. A Typical Feasibility Information Checklist for Materials Specification

Comment and or Conditions	YES or NO	Action Required
Does the "approved" source list include the intended material suppliers?		
Will the material suppliers be required to provide certification with each shipment?		
Have parameters to be checked in-house been identified?		
Are specified materials, heat treat and surface treatments compatible with the durability requirements in the intended environment?		

GAGE, FIXTURE, AND TEST EQUIPMENT

Special gages, fixtures, and test equipment are often required to test and inspect for significant and critical characteristics. These can be a fundamental requirement for determining a feasible quality product/process.

The design of each gage, fixture, and piece of test equipment is reviewed to determine if it effectively checks the variable characteristics of engineering specifications. It also verifies whether the special gages, fixtures, and test equipment have been subjected to repeatability and the ability to reproduce (Gage R & R) studies.

A typical sample of a feasibility information checklist for gage, fixture, and test equipment is shown in Table 16.

THE FINAL COMMITMENT: MANUFACTURING SIGN-OFF

A supplier must commit to its customer that a proposed product/process can be manufactured, assembled, packaged, and shipped in a final form that meets the customer's needs. The supplier is expected to seek out a method of manufacturing design product/process that is feasible, yet innovative, and can be produced:

- On commercially available equipment meeting production volumes and schedules

Table 16. A Typical Feasibility Information Checklist for Gage, Fixture, and Test Equipment

Comment and or Conditions	YES or NO	Action Required
Has the new equipment list been reviewed? Is it adequate?		
Can forecasted production volumes be met based upon the production capability of the equipment?		
Has preliminary process capability been established on the new equipment?		
Have gages for SPC been identified?		
Is the appropriate test equipment described in the ES available?		
Has the method of test equipment certification been established?		
Has the need for special gages and fixtures been identified and defined?		
Have special gages and fixtures received appropriate approvals?		
Are gage methods compatible between the customer's plant and the supplier?		
Are inspection gages and fixtures identified on the control plan?		
Have plans been made to conduct variation studies on measurement systems?		
Has correlation of all test equipment been established?		
Have scheduled calibration frequencies been established?		
Will machine potentials be established on the equipment builder's floor before delivery?		
When a nonconforming product is found, are there adequate test capabilities available to perform sufficient testing?		

- Giving consistent products that meet drawing tolerances and ES requirements
- Providing quality and reliability
- Supporting timing objectives
- Costing out effectively
- Meeting business plan objectives
- Being operationally efficient
- Bringing customer satisfaction
- Having a robust capable process
- Achieving a minimum C_{pk} on all significant and critical characteristics
- And if when produced, a C_{pk} of 1.33 is found in process, suggestions will be made to modify design product/process (if this is not possible, design product process is not feasible)
- For a prototype shop a P_{pk} with a value of 1.67 is more appropriate

Analytical techniques including design of experiments, design for manufacturing, and design for assembly are helpful in determining and selecting proper product/process design.

A typical manufacturing feasibility sign-off is shown in Table 17.

A typical assessment list of a manufacturing feasibility sign-off is shown in Table 18.

Table 17. A Typical Feasibility Information Checklist for Manufacturing Feasibility Sign-Off

Part Number	Part Name
Date	Notice

YES OR NO	Consideration
	Are you committed to the use of statistical process control for this product if awarded this business?
	Can all products be manufactured as specified on the drawings with a C_{pk} of at least 1.33 for all significant and critical characteristics?
	– Compatibility of specifications to accepted manufacturing standards
	– Containability to tolerance stack-up
	– Special equipment requirements
	– Adequacy of product definition to enable feasibility evaluation
	Can you meet the engineering specifications (ES) as written?
	– Containability of all ES requirements
	Can you meet the quality requirements of the customer?
	– Establishment of process capability at required volume
	– Maintenance of required quality system controls
	Can you meet all specified requirements at the projected volume level?
	– Adequacy of capacity. Has the process been fully analyzed to support production at the required volume and quality levels?
	Does the design allow use of conventional efficient material handling equipment and/or techniques?
	– Attainability of shipping densities
	Can the product be manufactured without incurring any unusual costs (capital equipment, tooling, or piece costs)?
	– Product improvement proposals
	– Cost reduction alternatives
	Do you presently employ statistical process control on similar products; are they in control?
	If in control, are they within the drawing tolerances with a C_{pk} of 1.33 or greater?

* ALL items with a "NO" answer must have an action plan

Table 18. A Typical Assessment List of a Manufacturing Feasibility Sign-Off

Item:	Number:	Comments
Feasible: Product can be produced as specified with no revisions: _____	Feasible: Changes recommended. Products can be improved or be less costly if proposed changes are incorporated:_____	
Marginally feasible: Changes recommended to achieve minimum C_{pk}:_____	Not feasible: Design revision recommended to produce product within the specified C_{pk} requirements: _____	
* ALL items checked as not feasible must have all changes identified in separate sheets.	* As a general rule, the assessment sheet is returned with a quotation and appropriate signatures from the supplier.	

REFERENCE

Stamatis, D.H. *Failure Mode and Effect Analysis: FMEA From Theory to Execution.* Milwaukee, WI: Quality Press, 1995.

SIX

Cost Accounting: Activity Based Costing (ABC)

The costs of doing business—labor, material, and overhead—cannot be effectively controlled without a system that effectively monitors how costs are incurred. Specifically, suppliers should develop standard costs, track the actual costs, and regularly compare the actual costs to their standard. The common methods currently used for cost accounting were developed between 1825 and 1925. Materials, labor, and overhead were the major categories for allocating manufacturing costs.

Today's accounting systems need to account for a significant problem in cost allocations. Cost allocations are generally calculated by dividing the number of direct labor hours into the overhead expense. Failure to evaluate the actual current cost of overhead by realistically viewing "hidden" organizational costs in the product/process has led to major pricing mistakes, including overcosts, as well as undercosts of particular products in manufacturing cost accounting. These mistakes account for unprofitable product/processes being developed and account for cost overrides that destroy profitability. Direct labor in today's manufacturing product/processes often accounts for anywhere from an average low of 5% to a high of 25%. Upwards of 50% of today's hidden costs include:

- Documentation
- Depreciation
- Engineering changes
- Rework
- Repair

Modern manufacturing economics dictate a change in standard cost accounting. Activity based accounting provides a sound alternative. The use of ABC measures is the consequence of changes in manufacturing, sales, customer service, complaint handling, quality issues, automation, and other areas (Huthwait, 1989). These systems cost a total product by looking at the following:

- Individual parts within the product
- Operation/processes that make up the part
- Direct costs—materials, direct labor, and tooling
- Indirect/hidden costs

Ledgers are used to view utility and loan agreements, budgets, quality control reports, and labor contracts. These activity-based systems identify, track, and assign costs to the source of the expense. The total life cycle costing allows companies to determine which products are truly profitable.

Cost accounting for the modern manufacturer should address the following questions:

- Is a standard cost accounting method serving you competitively in today's market?
- Is the accounting system for AQP and the design of the manufacturing product/process effectively providing the information needed to predict product/process profitability?
- Is the accounting system for AQP providing the information needed to determine appropriate and applicable profit margins?

- Is the method for tracing cost elements adequate?

- Is the run at rate as quoted?

- Is the organization assessing total life cycle costs for the product or missing "hidden" costs, such as telephone, fax, training, shipping, inspection, special expediting, mailing expenses, scrap expenses, part counts, retooling, or turnaround time?

- Is the organization assessing costs of the product/process by designing for manufacturing and giving your managers and engineers a chance to make effective decisions on assembly costs and time?

- Is the organization's utilization of manufacturing accounting data effective?

- Is your investigation and control of cost elements competitive? Is it possible to measure your success? Can you determine the real cause for poor performance, profit, sales, and customer service?

- Is your company utilizing new methods such as the cost of quality, cost of inventory, and cost of compliance?

- Is just-in-time having an effect on your financial system?

- Is there a real pay-off to seeking change in your cost accounting system?

Accounting and finance people must be teamed with the designer to identify and reduce the cost of product/processes. Accounting and finance is a vital member of an AQP team and is used to educate the designer to product/process lifecycle costs.

Changes in accounting and design philosophy can result in controlling continuous improvement. Real cost accounting of product/process is effective in producing to demand, reducing manufacturing lead time, striving for zero inventory and defects, reducing setup times, bringing cost reductions, and achieving on-time delivery.

To implement activity based accounting concepts, an integration of the areas of sales and marketing, engineering, planning, material control, production, quality, and administration must be accomplished. To effectively integrate these areas, it is necessary to redefine the role of cost management and gain management's support from the top down.

Top management is to set goals based on feedback from continuing operations, and to provide resources to departments to improve, at a minimum, the primary business goals of quality, cost, and delivery. Achieving the primary business goals will lead to customer satisfaction, and, ultimately, sustained profitability.

COST OF QUALITY

If the organization does not have the capability to develop a standard cost or an activity based cost system, then it should have at least a cost of quality system. A cost of quality system will provide the organization with information regarding

appraisal costs,

prevention costs,

internal failure costs, and

external failure costs.

These costs, individually and collectively, should be used by management for measurement, analysis, actions, and control. However, for an appropriate and truthful system that will identify the real costs in any organization, the element of fear must be removed and encouragement identifying the "real" costs should be rewarded. For more information on cost of quality see selected bibliography.

REFERENCE

Huthwait, B. "The Link Between Design and Activity Based Accounting." *Manufacturing Systems*. (1989): 44-47.

SEVEN

Prototype Development Tools: Customer-Driven Prototype Involvement

When the first essentially complete units of the product/ process are built and tested, tests to evaluate factors of basic design capability, environmental effects, and reliability for extended periods of operations are conducted. The adequacy of the basic design approach is being sought. If the product/process is not capable, the flaws are to be designed out now, not later (Juran, 1988).

AQP AND THE PROTOTYPE STAGE

AQP is aimed at excellence in serving the customer's needs. The prototype level of AQP programming is aimed at achieving continuous quality improvement through improved supplier process capability.

During AQP, process capability must be assessed on selected significant or critical characteristics. Modified initial sample report (ISR) and percentage of indexes with process capability/percentage of inspection points satisfying tolerance (PIPC/PIST) analysis is expected prior to shipment of prototype parts supporting the three major prototype builds:

1. EP, Evaluation Prototype

2. VP, Verification Prototype

3. FP, Functional Prototype

Decisions will be managed by facts that are supported by statistically valid, numeric data.

PROCEDURES FOR PROTOTYPES

In all prototype work the following general characteristics apply:

- Prototypes are usually the supplier's responsibility
- Modified ISR paperwork is required
- Capability studies and indexes are required where applicable and appropriate

  C_p/C_r

  C_{pk}

  P_p/P_{pk}

- A quality improvement plan is required for quality deficiencies
- A quality C_p/C_r form is issued at prototype builds

PLANNING FOR PROTOTYPE TOOLING CAPABILITY

Prototype tooling, rather than being a distinct and separate program, is now the beginning of the final production tooling program. Parts produced on prototype tooling are to be accompanied by capability projections for the customer and the supplier and designate significant/critical characteristics developed from short term capability studies. Prototype soft tooling is to have statistical capability support similar to hard tooling. If P_{pk} projections are less than 1.67, then appropriate and applicable plans should be prepared, so that the achievement of improved process capability can be reached.

C_{pks} or P_{pks} for parts produced on production tooling are to be determined if the parts are identical. X-bar & R charts may be used, if obtainable. Short-run SPC methodology should be used when appropriate and applicable. If traditional SPC methodology cannot be utilized, then use a 30 piece Process Potential Study of identical parts, or the 50/20 hour dry run test program, if applicable. On the other hand, if identical parts are not available, use prototype parts study.

On all prototype parts conduct the following (Ford, 1989).

1. Perform complete dimensional layouts of at least one part for each cavity or tool, but no less than six parts minimum.

2. For significant or critical characteristics with C_{pks} of less than 1.33, dimensions not to specifications, and/or non-normal distributions, provide plans to improve process capability.

3. Provide complete ES test results or timing completion dates where needed.

4. Submit deviations for all dimensions not to specification and all incomplete tests.

A typical review for tooling may include the following questions:

1. Have tools been certified to tool design print?

2. Have preproduction capability studies been conducted on tooling and machinery prior to acceptance at your company?

3. Have tools been numbered to be placed into your tool control program?

4. Have tooling set-up sheets and instructions been developed?

5. Have company maintenance personnel been make familiar with tooling maintenance training?

6. Have tooling capacity studies been conducted?

7. Is tooling capable of meeting daily, monthly, and weekly needs?

8. Is tooling made of material quality to sustain long-term product quality?

9. Have points for tooling capability studies been selected?

10. Will product capability studies be conducted on parts prior to tools being released to production?

11. Have you done similar parts before it is brought in for prototype production?

12. Is tooling paid for prior to capability analysis?

DEVIATIONS

Deviations are required for

any print dimension out of tolerance,

any material out of specification,

any engineering test out of specification, and

any engineering specification test which will not be completed by ISR and/or material review date (MRD).

MACHINE ACCEPTANCE

Suppliers who produce tooling and equipment must demonstrate accurately whether machine acceptance or rejection is documented appropriately. The basic considerations for a machine acceptance are:

Why:

To predict the ability of a machine to produce consistently to specification

To analyze operations producing outside specification limits

Machine capability is always a prerequisite for process capability

How:

By statistical analysis of data gathered from a representative sample

Through actual applications

When:

Prior to taking delivery of new process equipment

Before approving newly installed process equipment for production use

Where:

In equipment suppliers' plant(s)

In company manufacturing and or assembly plant(s)

In outside suppliers' manufacturing plants

What:

Characteristics required by customer

Characteristics chosen by the equipment supplier or the manufacturing assembly activity

Who:

Customer project engineer and machine builder—design and construction of a capable machine or process

Quality assurance/control—verification of machine or process capability

A typical approach for machine acceptance has three phases:

PHASE 1. The goal of Phase 1 is to stabilize machine performance to ensure that the machine is running to specification. Statistically, this means ensuring that only one distribution is present, centering that distribution at a target value, and reducing process variability around that target.

PHASE 2. The goal of Phase 2 is to establish preliminary control limits to be used in Phase 3. Verification of Phase 1 goals will also be accomplished using a larger sample size, if applicable and appropriate.

PHASE 3. The goal of Phase 3 is to establish short-term machine capability at designated machine speed over a minimum of a predetermined time limit by control charting as the study is in progress.

A typical checklist for a machine acceptance is shown in Table 19.

Table 19. Potential Machine Acceptance Checklist

Comments/Conditions	Yes	No	Actions Required
Conducting the Study			
Have all measuring devices been calibrated?			
Were correcting adjustments made before study?			
Are parts marked and results recorded in sequence?			
Have unusual occurrences been recorded in a log?			
Was machine operated to an approved process?			
Were adjustments locked in to prevent drift?			
Have provisions been made to measure a minimum of 30 pieces?			
Is measurement precision at least one-tenth specification tolerance?			
Interpretation of results			
If the process average and plus or minus 4s are not within the engineering specification tolerances, consider the following:			
Is the problem in the average?			
Is the problem in the range?			
Is there something unique about the pieces with the smallest values, the largest values, or both?			
Was there any trend or pattern to the data over the time of the study?			
Does the histogram suggest any unusual conditions such as non-normality?			
Does the log show any unusual occurrences that would help explain apparent incapability?			
Should the study be rerun?			

MACHINE CAPABILITY ANALYSIS

Machine capability studies on both new and existing operations are to be used to prove capability by the supplier. These studies are recommended at the original equipment manufacturer, at installation, and periodically throughout machine life.

Determining process capability is a combination of the performance of machine capability studies followed up with process potential studies. The verification of machines' capability and process capability is vital to the protection of the investment that is made in process equipment.

Manufacturing engineering and the machine builder are responsible for the design and construction of machines and processes that are capable of meeting specifications over the long run, and the submission of these machines and processes for capability analysis. Quite often, quality control is responsible for verifying capability and assisting in the diagnosis of non-capability.

A machine capability study is a short-term analysis of less than 30 days (typically it is a few minutes to a few days). The analysis is performed on a single machine/tool and measures tooling and equipment related variability. The purpose of a short-term machine capability study is to calculate the potential for realizing long-term capability.

Performance criteria for machine capability analysis are much more demanding. This stringency is to allow room for the variability that is to be introduced by other process elements and/or time related factors. A result 99.94% (+ or - 4 sigma) within specification is expected, or there is minimal opportunity for achieving the goal of at least 99.74% (+ or - 3 sigma) process capability over the long term.

PROCESS POTENTIAL STUDIES

The process potential study is similar to the machine capability study. As an intermediate level of study, it analyzes short-term process capability. Basically, it is a short-term estimate of whether a process as a whole is likely to meet a customer's long-term quality requirements. The estimate is based on limited samples and a limited production history. The study requirements may differ; however, the data from a process potential study and a machine capability analysis can be interpreted by the same basic methods. At production date, an estimated process capability is to be proven from identical, similar, related, or new processes.

Keep in mind that machine capability analysis and process potential studies have the final goal of long-term product/process performance; in other words, the mingling of machine capability and continuing product/process control.

To use C_p or C_{pk} for ongoing processes, using X-bar & R charts or 30-piece potential data, the production process must have variable data and be in statistical control. It is essential that a process potential study be conducted for all customer or supplier significant characteristics on components. Estimates for long-range C_p and C_{pk} may be used as three-quarters of the short range C_p, C_{pk} values, which are based on three sigma estimates.

Again, it must be emphasized that if the C_{pk} index is not applicable, then the P_p or P_{pk} or parts per million (ppm) should be used.

A P_p is an index similar to C_p but based on data from early, short-term studies of a new process. P_p can be calculated only when the data from the study indicate that process stability has been achieved. Similarly, a P_{pk} index is similar to C_{pk} but based on data from early, short-term studies of new processes. Data from at least 20 subgroups are required for preliminary assessments. P_{pk} can be calculated only when the data from the study indicate that stability has been achieved. (Both P_p and P_{pk} are excellent indexes for capability in the tooling and equipment industry as well as for processes with limited data.)

Using PIST/PIPC

At least with Ford Motor Company, at the prototype level, in addition to statistical proof of process/product capability, a modified ISR and PIPC/PIST (PIST is the percentage of inspection points that are within the tolerances indicated on the design drawing. It is a quality benchmark.) analysis is required. These items are needed prior to shipment of prototype parts supporting the three major prototype builds:

1. EP, Evaluation Prototype

2. VP, Verification Prototype

3. FP, Functional Prototype

PIST equals the number of conforming inspection points divided by total inspection points multiplied by 100%.

PIPC is a percentage of critical or significant characteristics with C_p indexes greater than or equal to 1.00 in the prototype phase. At the production phase, the percentage of critical or significant characteristics with C_p and C_{pk} indexes is to be greater than or equal to 1.33. Using capability indexes gives a knowledge of the quality level of your parts.

Use the results to complete ISR forms at the prototype stage. PIPC equals the number of process potential studies with a minimum of 1.33 C_p, C_{pk} divided by the total number of studies multiplied by 100%.

Comments on C_{pk} Targets

Even though over the last several years the C_{pk} has gained some notoriety in the quality world, there are still some misunderstandings about it as well as shortcomings.

To consider a capability with a C_{pk} index, one must have a normally distributed process, a consistent process, and a process in statistical control. If these conditions exist, then the process is a predictable process and a C_{pk} is appropriate. If these conditions do not exist, then the C_{pk} is not an appropriate measure of capability. If the C_{pk} is not applicable, other measures such as P_p or P_{pk} may be used, or even ppm (parts per million) may be considered.

By definition a C_{pk} measures the dispersion of the distribution in relation to the target, which of course is the goal. To do that, this capability index is derived from two metrics, namely the specification and the process variability. Therefore, the index can be changed by changing either of the metrics. Most corporate objectives include a reduction of variability (one of the capability components) as the predominant goal of their quality efforts. This obviously should be encouraged and should be an overriding consideration in dealing with quality issues. However, by placing undue emphasis on C_p or C_{pk}, we run the risk of having our component supply base (both internal and external) and our equipment suppliers misinterpret our objective as attaining a specific C_p or C_{pk} ratio, by any means, rather than continuous improvement.

We can simply state that we want to measure stability (process control charts) and then assess process variability (process capability). By focusing on the process variability we can prevent the misinterpretation of our goals.

In order to clarify the issues with C_{pk}, the exact meaning of this index must be quantified. A $C_{pk} = 1.0$ means that we are plus or minus 3σ capable, or that 99.73% of the parts are within bilateral specifications. A $C_{pk} = 1.33$ means that we are plus or minus 4σ capable, or that 99.994% of the parts are within bilateral specifications. To put it differently, a $C_{pk} = 1.0$ means 2,699 defects per million parts (dppm) and a $C_{pk} = 1.33$ means 63 dppm. It is obvious from this quantification that attribute measures are extremely inefficient for measuring capabilities of these magnitudes. For example, a p chart can be used to demonstrate capability for $C_{pk} = 1.0$ only if a minimum sample size of 1,900 parts are used for each point on the p chart and if a minimum of 25 points are in control—this requires 47,500 total parts to demonstrate capability. Likewise for $C_{pk} = 1.33$, the same control must be demonstrated, but each sample must be a minimum of 79,400 parts and a total of 1,985,000 will be used to demonstrate capability.

A final note. C_{pk} can only have positive values. It will equal zero when the actual process average matches or falls outside one of the specification limits. The C_{pk} can never be greater than the C_p, only equal to it. This happens when the actual process average falls in the middle of the specification limit.

REFERENCE

Ford Motor Company. *Supplier Quality Improvement Guidelines for Prototypes*. Dearborn, MI: North America Automotive Operations (NAAO) Purchasing. (March 1989): 44-46.

Juran, J.M. *Juran's Quality Control Handbook*. 4th ed. NewYork, NY: McGraw Hill. (1988) 13.5-13.6.

EIGHT

Manufacturing Preparedness: Preparing Product for Manufacturing

Meeting customer needs, producing high quality, and designing products well are reliant on the development of a comprehensive and effective manufacturing system. When product/process manufacturing begins, the objective of the AQP teams is to continue a manufacturing system that ensures the design requirements of the customer are met and understood. Implementation and control of the manufacturing product/processes is crucial. Scrutinizing and confirming manufacturing capability always remain the assignment of the AQP team.

THE FLOW CHART AS A QUALITY TOOL

Defining the process is important to process control. Understanding the process itself is vital. To control a process, one must identify what is significant to manufacturing and production of the product/process. One way to help understand and define the process is a flow chart. The flow chart is a pictorial representation of the process.

It may include

floor layout,

proposed stops,

transport methods,

each process step with the critical or significant characteristics, and

identification of current controls.

The communicating language of a flow chart is pictures, engineering symbols, and geometric shapes, all of which illustrate the process. To construct a flow chart of a product/process, the correct make-up of participants must be present. The following list of participants is suggested to start developing a flow chart:

- Those who work with the process (they are the process owners)
- Suppliers to the process
- Customers of the process
- Supervisor of the process function area
- Independent facilitator

As a general rule, the flow chart may be constructed by both the core and extended team members. Because at this stage there are many participants, it is very important for the facilitator to make sure that all flow chart team members participate on an equal level. Team members are to discuss and chart the process. The facilitator is to keep focus on the team objective and to write down the information that enters into the creation of the process flow chart.

As the discussion progresses, displaying the chart as it is created is recommended, so that all team members can see its component parts at all times. A very large blackboard or, better yet, a roll of non-plasticized shelf liner paper is a good way

Figure 9—A typical flow chart showing the relationship of the FMEA in the APQP process.

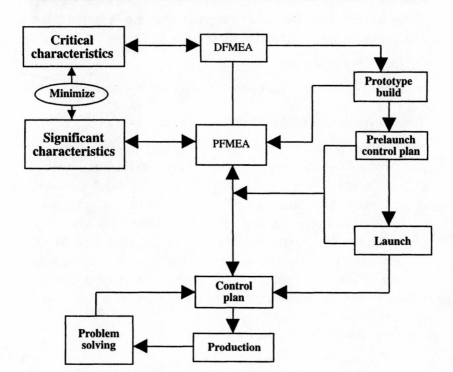

to display the chart as it develops. Remember, a record of the results must be maintained.

It is not unusual if developing a flow chart takes several sessions. To be sure, it is time consuming, but very important because the time spent to investigate the process and analyze the chart for missing steps is essential for future decisions about the process. The importance of this activity demands open discussion of the process flow with both positive and negative input. On the other hand, it is just as important to avoid personal, negative, and defensive questions.

From an AQP perspective, in a flow chart first the *what* aspect of the phase currently being worked on is addressed, then the *when* aspect. Once that is done, moving to the activity matrix, the *who* is tied to the *what*. An activity matrix is a tool for understanding organizational interactions for any given activity, based on what happens and who is responsible. The purpose of the activity matrix is to

identify process owners and

identify functions that provide inputs and outputs.

THE CONTROL CHART AS A QUALITY TOOL

Accomplishing the regulation of manufacturing capability on the production floor is contingent on establishing control plans. The flow chart is a first step towards the development of control plans. Once the process flow is determined, it is easier to develop control plans that promote quality products beginning with the pre-production manufacturing product/ process.

A control plan focuses on product, process, and inspection requirements for a particular product. The quality system encompasses the fundamentals needed to control and maintain the product quality.

The essentials of a quality system are:

- Control of supplier products

- Manufacturing process capability

- Statistical process control

- Inspection and laboratory test inspection instructions

- Measuring and testing equipment

- Engineering performance testing

- Product qualification and lot sampling

- Control of non-conforming products

- Layout inspection

- Drawing and change control

- Quality system and product performance records

Suppliers are to determine that the proposed control plan is capable of operating within the existing quality systems, and that the plan is representative of the company's policies, procedures, and practices.

IDENTIFY CONTROL ITEMS AND CRITICAL AND SIGNIFICANT CHARACTERISTICS

Control items and significant or critical characteristics are identified from a review of the design and/or process FMEAs.

Identify Control Items

Control items are parts that can affect either compliance with government regulations or safe product/process operation, and are identified by the customer's product engineering on drawings and specifications with a specific and unique symbol. Some of the typical symbols are inverted delta, shield, and diamond. (for example, Ford uses the inverted delta for critical characteristics, preceding the part number).

Identify Significant Characteristics

Significant and critical characteristics are those product, process, and test characteristics for which quality planning actions must be summarized on control plans, such as:

- Characteristics are identified by the producer, customer quality engineer, design engineer, and product engineer on the basis of product/process knowledge.

- The characteristics can be critical or significant to the quality, reliability, durability, fit, or function of the product/process.

- Characteristics are to be identified on prints, specifications, or quality plans.

In addition, significant and critical characteristics may be identified as the characteristics that affect profitability, such as

cycle time,

delivery time, and

high warranty claims items.

Identify Critical Characteristics

Critical characteristics are determined by customer product engineering and apply to a component's material, assembly, or product assembly operation. These items are designated by customer engineering as being critical to part function and having particular quality, reliability, and durability significance. Critical characteristics are identified by the use of specific symbols and are designated by the customer.

For example, the method of designation of control characteristics by General Motors may include identification on the drawing's specifications, reliability orders, reliability directives, or purchased quality standards (PQS), or through programs such as failure prevention analysis (FPA), failure mode and effects analysis (FMEA), or others that are specific to a particular General Motor's division. In any case, control characteristics are to be identified so that appropriate statistical methods may be implemented.

PROCESS FMEA, A DISCIPLINED REVIEW/ANALYSIS QUALITY TOOL

The process FMEA is a problem solving tool used to eliminate problems from production systems prior to the official production release (process design) date for the product/processes. Process FMEAs are to be used for all new processes and/or changed processes. A typical process FMEA form is shown in Figure 10.

Process FMEAs identify potential process concerns and the actions needed to eliminate them. The process FMEA is to be prepared by the manufacturing engineering team prior to the commencement of tooling. Ideally, however, although not mandatory, a design FMEA is made available during the preparation of the process FMEA.

A review of the design FMEA to determine severity ratings is conducted by the design engineer. The design FMEA is not a precondition for a process FMEA, and the lack of a design FMEA is never a good enough excuse to delay the development of a process FMEA. However, the information gained

Figure 10—A typical process FMEA form.

Potential Failure Mode and Effect Analysis (FMEA) (Process Form)

System _____
Process _____
Item _____
Model _____

Process responsibility _____
Due Date _____
Core Team _____

FMEA Number _____
Page _____ of _____
Prepared by _____
FMEA date: Original _____ Revised _____

Purpose/ Function and/or Requirements	Potential Failure Mode	Potential Effect(s) of Failure	S E V	Potential Cause(s) Mechanism(s) of Failure	O C C U R	Current Process Controls	D E T E C	R P N	Recommended Action(s)	Responsibility and Target Completion Date	ACTION RESULTS			
											Action Taken	S E V	O C C	D E T
														R P N

from the design FMEA can be very important to the process/ manufacturing process FMEA team.

An FMEA is required by all automotive companies, and its use is expanding in other industries as well. The application of an FMEA is expected for all new processes and/or changed processes. Furthermore, it is expected to be done in the early stages of quality planning of the product/process and with the understanding that it is going to be updated as needed. After all, the FMEA is a dynamic and evolving document. In order to comply with the FMEA requirements, the reader is encouraged to see Chrysler, Ford, General Motors (1995), and Stamatis (1995) for the application, examples, form, and the interpretation of FMEA.

> *Special note:* As of late, there are some automotive companies not using the RPN as a measure of priority in the application of both the design and process FMEA. Instead, they use only the severity and occurrence. The rationale for this is that the RPN can be manipulated by the team.

We strongly disagree with this trend for two reasons. First, by definition, FMEA is a tool that prioritizes the failure based on occurrence, severity, and detection. To alter this configuration changes the mechanics of the FMEA. If indeed manipulation of the RPN is a problem, then appropriate training is required, not changing the mechanics of the tool. Second, to exclude the detection is a serious oversight, because detection relates the failure directly to the customer. The omission can be very costly.

Control Plan as a Quality Tool

The purpose of the control plan methodology is to aid in the manufacture of quality products according to customer requirements. It does this by providing a structured approach for the design, selection, and implementation of value-added control methods for the total system. As a consequence, all types of control plans are considered to be "controlled docu-

Figure 11—A typical control plan form.

Original Date: _____

Revised Date: _____

Authorization: _____

Prepared by: _____

Page: _____ of _____

Process: _____

Flowchart	Critical Characteristics	Class	Sample Size and Frequency	Inspection or Test Procedure	Control Method	Gage Description, Master, Detail	Report Document	Additional Requirements	Other Information	Reaction Plan

ments." The control plan is a written summary that describes the method(s) and tool(s) that the process is using, so that variation is minimized. There are many ways to develop a control plan. However, in the automotive industry, there is a standard form that the suppliers should follow. The guidelines and specific examples for the automotive approach to control plans may be found in Chrysler, Ford, and General Motors (1995b).

Regardless of what form is used, the intent of a control plan is to provide the flow and documentation of the methodology used in the process, to minimize variation due to special causes. (A typical control plan form is shown in Figure 11 and a typical control plan with an FMEA is shown in Figure 12.) The control plan does not replace the information contained in detailed operator instructions; rather, it supplements it, especially in the area of quality activities, such as: when to use sampling; how much sampling is necessary; the frequency of inspection; the specific usage of SPC. This methodology is applicable to a wide range of manufacturing and non-manufacturing processes and technologies. The control plan is an integral part of an overall quality process and is to be utilized as a living document. Therefore, the control plan is not a tool that should be used in a vacuum. Rather, it should be used in conjunction with other quality-related documents.

Because the control plan is the map for all quality activities at the production job level, it is imperative that all operators know of its existence and physical location. Therefore, the actual control plan document must be in the proximity of the process it identifies and controls, and its contents must be familiar to all the operators who come in contact with that process.

Perhaps one of the most important aspects of utilizing a control plan is its construction. A single control plan may apply to a group or family of products that are produced by the same process at the same source, as long as it addresses the process issues and concerns for controlling the process itself and its parts. A typical control plan may be written, but also it may be augmented with prints, sketches, and anything

Figure 12—A typical control plan with an FMEA.

Company: ______	Part Name: ______	Authorized Control Plan by: ______
Division/Plant: ______	Part Number: ______	Authorized FMEA by: ______
Department: ______	Control Plan Orig. Date: ______	Control Plan Leader: ______
Process: ______	FMEA Orig. Date: ______	FMEA Leader: ______
Operation: ______	Control Plan Rev. Date: ______	FMEA Members: ______
Machine: ______	FMEA Rev. Date: ______	
Station: ______	Page ______ of ______ Pages	

Char #	Characteristic Description (product & process)	Spec	TYPE	IMP	FAILURE MODE	Effects of Failure	SEV	Causes of failure	OCC	CURRENT CONTROLS	DET	RPN	RECOM. ACTIONS	ACTIONS TAKEN	SEV	OCC	DET	RPN	RESPONSIBLE PERSON	Ctrl. Fact	CLASS	Control Method	TOOL	Gage, desc., master, detail	Other *

*** Typical other items may include:**

GR & R & Date	Cp/Cpk (target) & Date	Reaction plans	Inspection require-ments	Sampling requirements

else that enhances its use and applicability. Of course, for maximizing the control plan's utility, process monitoring instructions should be provided and used continually.

Because of the versatility of the control plan and its ability to describe the actions that are required at each phase of the process (however that process is defined), it is not unusual to find a control plan in receiving, in-process for periodic requirements to assure that all process outputs will be in a state of control, and out-going. During the in-process regular production run, the control plan provides the process monitoring and control method(s) that will be used to control both critical and significant characteristics. Since processes are expected to be continually updated and improved, the control plan reflects a strategy that is responsive to these changing process conditions and, as a consequence, the control plan is a continual improvement tool as well as a control document.

The control plan is maintained and used throughout the product life cycle. Early in the product life cycle its primary purpose is to document and communicate the initial plan for process control. Subsequently, it guides manufacturing in how to control the process and ensure product quality. Ultimately, the control plan remains a living document reflecting the current methods of control and measurement. The control plan is updated as measurement systems and control methods are evaluated and improved. As these changes are occurring, the control plan becomes a dynamic tool and, at this stage, it is called a dynamic control plan.

DYNAMIC CONTROL PLAN (DCP)

What is DCP? The acronym DCP stands for dynamic control plan. DCP is a methodology to ensure that the customer expectations in the form of product design requirements are understood, deployed, and controlled in the manufacturing and assembly processes. The dynamic control plan describes the actions required at each phase of the process to assure all parts produced will be uniform and conform to the customers

Figure 13—Dynamic control plan.

Dynamic Control Plan

Department:
Operation #:
Process:
Engineer:
(1)

Part Name:
Base Part Number:
(2)

Page _____ of _____
Issue Date:
Revision #:
(3)

DCP ID # (4)	Characteristic Description and Specification (5)	Type (6)	Control Factor (7)	Class (8)	Control Method (9)	Sampling Frequency, Size & Master Freq. (10)	Gage Description Gage Number Master Number (11)	Reaction Plans (12)

Type: IP=In Process; FIP=Finish in Process; BP=Finish Blueprint
Control Factors: M=Machine; T=Tool; C=Component; S=Setup; F=Fixture; O=Operator; E=Environment;
P=Preventive Maintenance (13)

Control Copies
#1 = Eng. Office
#2 = Process (14)

satisfaction. In the most simplest terms, a DCP is a combination of an FMEA and a control plan, utilizing a single form.

The DCP is a living document, which means that it is subject to revision. That these revisions are discussed and agreed upon through each department's DCP team participating in DCP meetings. An example of a DCP is shown in Figure 13. The form in the DCP example is coded with numerical values from 1-12. Each number has a special meaning and is explained here.

1. Department, operation number, name of the process, and the engineer responsible for the last update.

2. Part name and base part number.

3. Pagination. Issue date refers to the original date of the process. The revision number shows how many updates have occurred since the issue date.

4. DCP dimension number from the blueprint.

5. Characteristic description and specification.

(Special Note for Items 4 and 5: The information in these two columns must match with the process illustration if there is one)

6. Appropriate abbreviations are listed to indicate the characteristic status at each phase of the operation. Typical abbreviations are: IP = In-process (characteristic)—other steps in the process will affect or change this characteristic before it is completed; FIP = Finished in-process—the characteristic will not be affected or changed after this step in the process. The difference between FIP and BP is that the customer will not see this particular characteristic. For example, a locating surface used early in the process, that becomes non-existent by the time the product leaves the area; BP = Finished blueprint—the characteristic will not be affected or changed after this step in the process. The specification described meets or exceeds those on the blueprint or customer specifications.

7. Code item for the control factor. Typical codes are:
F = Fixture/pallet dominant—the fixture or pallets holding
the parts are the greatest source of inconsistency;
M = Machine dominant—the machine producing the
characteristic is the greatest source of inconsistency;
C = Component dominant—incoming component nonconformity is the primary source of product variability;
S = Setup dominant—the characteristic is highly repro-
ducible once the proper setup has occurred; T = Tool
dominant—the characteristic is uniform but drifts over
time from tool wear; O = Operator dominant—unifor-
mity of the characteristic is highly dependent on
operator skill; P = Preventive Maintenance dominant—
process consistency is dependent upon scheduled
maintenance activities; E = Environment dominant—
the characteristic is susceptible to environmental
conditions.

8. Characteristic classification. The characteristic classification is the process for categorizing characteristics
for the purposes of control planning. The following
characteristics are typical. Critical characteristics (CC):
part or process requirements (dimensions, specifications,
tests, processes, assembly sequences, tooling, torque,
welds, attachments, component usages, and so on)
which affect government regulatory compliance for safe
vehicle/product function and require specific supplier,
manufacturing, assembly, shipping, monitoring, and/or
inspection actions. CCs are further identified with a
special symbol, such as an inverted delta or the
company's specific identification mark or symbol. This
special symbol is expected to be found on customers'
drawings, control plans, and product and stock identification tags. Significant characteristics (SC): catego-
rized characteristics of products, processes, and tests,
where a reduction in variation, within a specified
tolerance, around a proper target will improve customer satisfaction. High impact characteristics (HIC):
product or process characteristics that, when outside

the specification tolerance, severely affect subsequent manufacturing operations or customer satisfaction. However, the product or process *is not* unsafe. High impact characteristics may be defined through quality history, manufacturer profile engineering profile, and performance versus targets. Other characteristics (other): all characteristics not classified as CC, SC, or HIP. *(Note: ALL CCs and SCs must be control charted.)*

9. Method of controlling the process. For variable data, control charts, such as X-bar and R charts, are expected. For attribute data, control charts, such p, np, c, and u charts are recommended. Other methods are also acceptable, depending on the process. Other typical methods are: check sheet, operational definitions, and DOE.

10. Specific inspection practices. An example is: sampling, its frequency and the size. It is very important to identify here "when" and "how many." It is not necessary to identify the setup verification samples. In this column it is also mandatory to identify the "mastering frequency." Mastering frequency is the process of validating the master gage. Therefore, it is imperative in this column to identify how often the gage is to be mastered.

11. Specific gage as a means of measuring or testing and its respective master. Gages may be referred to by a descriptive name, such as plug gage. Most gage numbers, at this location, begin with 00-XY or whatever the system may be, followed with a group of numbers, such as 00-XY-14567. Most gage masters, at this location, begin with 00-AB or whatever the system may be, and then followed with a group of numbers, such as 00-AB-1234. Additional extensions of the gage may be referred to as a detail, such as 11-ST- 12345 Det. A.

Figure 14—Dynamic control plan: Question log.

Dynamic Control Plan: Question Log

Department:
Date:
Part Name:
Part Number:

Team Members:

Priority	#	Open Date	Asked by	Question or Issue	Answered by	Date Due	Status	Status Date	Answer or Resolution	Close Date

12. Reaction plan(s). A reaction plan is the action speci-
    fied when nonconforming product or process instabil-
    ity is identified. This action is in the form of
    "corrective action" and "containment procedures"
    which have been established for each characteristic
    in the event of a nonconforming occurrence.

13. Legend for type, control factors, and characteristic
    classification. Typical entries are: **Type:** IP = In-
    process, FIP = Finish In-process, BP = Finish blue-
    print; **Control Factors:** M = Machine, T = Tool,
    C = Component, S = Setup, F = Fixture, O = Operator,
    E = Environment, P = Preventive Maintenance.

14. Information for document control . The first copy
    resides with the engineer. The second copy resides
    with the process. The date printed refers to the last
    time the control plan was updated.

In conjunction with the DCP, sometimes a question log is
used (see Fig. 14). A question log tracks open issues and maintains a history of knowledge gained. It provides support
throughout all DCP activities and it answers the question,
"Are the teams moving forward?" It is specifically used to:

- Coordinate team activities
- Record open questions, issues, and concerns
- Capture ideas for future consideration
- Track progress and record knowledge gained

For a DCP to be effective and productive it must be recognized up front that there are some roles and responsibilities
by the supervisors and or advisors. These are:

- The leadership must be shared. The leader of DCP and
  the process engineer must work together
- Ensure DCP meetings are held regularly, as defined by
  the organization's quality system
- Ensure DCP team members are reminded of meeting
  time and location

- Review DCPs at meetings for updates and process changes
- Control meeting and build teamwork
- Maintain team focus
- Act as team spokesperson
- Organize team guide progress
- Keep #1 controlled copy of department DCP
- Ensure DCP has been reviewed and signed off
- Ensure that all department personnel know where to find the DCP
- Ensure that all department personnel have had DCP training

Note: All types of control plans, including the DCP, should be changed, modified, or revised when appropriate. Actions that demand a review for such changes, modifications, and/or revisions include the following:

- Process changed and/or modified
- Product change and/or modified
- Customer requirements changed, modified, or revised
- Testing and/or inspection procedures changed, modified, or revised
- Sampling methodology changed, modified, or revised

EMPLOYEE INSTRUCTIONS AS A QUALITY TOOL

All operating personnel need written process monitoring instructions. The written instructions are developed from the following documents (Stamatis, 1996; 1997).

- FMEAs and the control plan
- Engineering drawings, performance specifications, material specifications, and industry standards
- Supplier expertise and knowledge of the processes and products
- Handling of the product

Employees need process monitoring instructions. The process monitoring instructions may include:

- Process sheets
- Inspection and laboratory test instructions
- Shop travelers
- Test procedures
- Equipment setup and operating instructions
- Control plan
- Other documents necessary for monitoring and operating the process

For example, process sheets might describe the production operation sequence including significant characteristics and process control applications. Process flow charts are often effective due to their visual nature. Use of pictorial and cartoon instructions are particularly effective on the production floor. Instructions should include information on what to do, how to do it, how to recognize change in the product or process, and what action to take.

Instructions are to be posted at the work station or made available in a manual, preferably a ring binder for ease of change. Detailed process monitoring information is to be accessible for reference by both operator and supervisor.

It is the quality planning team's duty to develop, review, and verify that adequate and complete instructions are available for control and verification purposes during any process/product manufacturing activity.

PROCESS CAPABILITY AS A QUALITY TOOL

Process capability is the measured, inherent reproducibility of the product turned out by the process (Juran, 1988). To understand the concept of capability, it helps to look at the associated definitions:

- *Process* refers to a combination of machine, tools, methods, measurement, environment, materials, and people producing a product/process.

- *Capability* refers to the competence of the product/ process. Competence in the product/process is determined by testing performance and measuring the results. The product as the end result is measured for variation.

- *Inherent reproducibility* is a uniform product/process that is considered to be in statistical control and has a lack of variation in its production.

- *Machine capability* refers to capability determined under short-term study with one operator and uniform raw materials, manufacturing conditions, and practices.

- *Process capability* refers to capability over a long period of time with changes in workers, material, and other process conditions.

A useful AQP procedure should produce a product/process that is both stable and capable. A capability study on the product/process is effective when the new process is conducted preliminary to a full production run. The preliminary process capability study will be of limited duration and cannot fully represent long-term production capability. However, capable performance can indicate whether room for improvement exists at this stage.

Process capability studies can be conducted in the equipment supplier's plant. This study will reflect equipment problems, but will not indicate the effect of eventual production floor operating conditions. A second study can be conducted to reflect floor conditions upon delivery and installation at the facility of operation. Finally, process capability is to be conducted during ongoing production to determine long-run process stability and capability. At each stage, analysis of the study should be made to determine actions which could result in *continual improvement* of the product/process. A typical preliminary process capability study checklist is shown in Table 20.

PREPARATION FOR STUDY

A typical preparation preliminary process capability study checklist is shown in Table 21.

Table 20. A Typical Preliminary Process Capability Study Checklist

Concern	Action needed: YES OR NO	What is the Action?	Comments
Has the team developed the plan?			
Have influencing factors been identified?			
Has the extent of the study been determined?			
Is the run long enough and are conditions suitable for determining sources of variation?			
Is the data collection method compatible with the analysis method and the goals of the study?			
Is the plan ready prior to the run?			

Table 21. A Typical Preparation Preliminary Process Capability Study Checklist

Concern	Action needed: YES OR NO	What is the Action?	Comments
Calibrate and evaluate the measurement process for stability.			
Check measurements system for a tolerance of $1/10$ the width or better in measurement.			
Check gage system error for acceptable criteria.			
Check if the trial run ran according to plan.			
Check if unusual adjustments or events were logged.			
Check if measurements were noted and identified with parts.			
Check if parts were kept for diagnostic purposes for future plans.			

ANALYZE DATA COLLECTION

A typical preliminary process capability study checklist to analyze the data is shown in Table 22.

Table 22. A Typical Preliminary Process Capability Study Checklist to Analyze the Data

Concern	Action needed: YES OR NO	What is the Action?	Comments
Check if an appropriate method is being used to evaluate stability and that it is understood.			
Check if the process is stable for both average (location) and range (variation).			
Check if the statistical evidence makes sense in relation to event log and process knowledge.			
Check for evidence of warm-up, tool wear, material changes, etc.			
Check method for suitability for evaluating potential capability and see if it is understood.			
Check the process for potential capability with regard to guidelines or customer requirements.			

ACTION PLAN QUESTIONS

A typical preliminary process capability study checklist to analyze the action plan concerns is shown in Table 23.

Table 23. A Typical Preliminary Process Capability Study Checklist to Analyze the Action Plan Concerns

Concern	Action needed: YES OR NO	What is the Action?	Comments
Are there opportunities to improve process performance?			
Are specific actions being taken to solve problems of instability or lack of potential capability?			
Has the study been rerun to confirm effectiveness?			
If performance for process capability is not acceptable, has a plan for improvement been adopted?			
Has specification relief been considered? Is it justified?			
Should product/process design be changed?			
Is output to be sorted?			

FINAL RESPONSE TO STUDY

What is the *action plan* resulting from the *process capability* study that will provide continual improvement during long-term production?

REFERENCE

Chrysler, Ford, and General Motors. *Failure Mode and Effect Analysis.* Chrysler, Ford and General Motors. Distributed by the Automotive Industry Action Group. Southfield, MI, 1995a.

Chrysler, Ford, and General Motors. *Advanced Product Quality Planning and Control Plan.* Chrysler, Ford and General Motors. Distributed by the Automotive Industry Action Group. Southfield, MI, 1995b.

Juran, J.M. *Juran's Quality Control Handbook.* 4th ed. New York, NY: McGraw Hill. (1988): 13.5-13.6.

Stamatis, D.H. *TQM Engineering Handbook.* New York, NY: Marcel Dekker, Inc., 1997.

Stamatis, D.H. *Documenting and Auditing for ISO 9000 and QS-9000: Tools for Ensuring Certification or Registration.* Chicago, IL: Irwin Professional Publishing, 1996.

Stamatis, D.H. *Failure Mode and Effect Analysis: FMEA From Theory to Execution.* Milwaukee, WI: Quality Press, 1995.

NINE

Selected Analytical Techniques Used in the Course of AQP

There are many tools that can be used in the process of conducting an advanced quality planning program. The actual applicability and appropriateness of each of the tools should be the guide for selection as the "right" tool. In this chapter we will identify some of the most frequently used tools, without the implication that these are the best or most important. In addition, we also will identify some of the expected inputs and outputs from each of the five phases of AQP.

GAGE R & R: A QUALITY MEASUREMENT TOOL

Suppliers are responsible for developing a gage measurement verification system. The importance of the gages used to control processes and evaluate material conformance is not to be underestimated. The AQP team is responsible to develop a plan for a quality measurement system.

An adequate gage control system includes (Chrysler, Ford, and General Motors, 1995a):

- Design and certification
- Capability assessment (over time)

- Mastering
- Operational definition
- Control
- Repair and recertification

One or more tests are to be conducted to determine if the system is appropriate. The test assessment is usually done in two phases: 1) Testing is performed to determine if the measurement system has the statistical properties needed to perform the needed measurements. 2) Periodic retesting is done to learn if the measurement system is satisfactory.

Gage accuracy is necessary to validate the variation in measurement that is done for statistical process control (SPC). Without validation, inconsistencies and incorrect measurements for variation can cause costly misdirected decisions. Validation is to be against recognized standards, or masters and their traceability is required. If the gages are determined to be outside the predetermined limits, corrective action on the gage and affected material is to be logged. Master gages are to be validated to established standards (e.g., National Institute of Standards and Technology [NIST]) and certification regarding accuracy is to be at specified intervals. Gages, jigs, fixtures, templates, and patters, used as measurement devices, are to be inspected at established intervals and identified to the latest engineering change. Computerized gages need written procedures that define the frequency, control, and verification of acceptance limits.

Measurement systems are to be assessed periodically for repeatability, reproducibility, accuracy, stability, and linearity. Three areas are to be considered when evaluating a measurement system.

1. Does the measurement system have adequate discrimination? Can it really discriminate between "good" and "bad" parts?

2. Is the measurement system statistically stable over time? Is the measurement system consistent?

3. Is the measurement error (variation) small? Depending on the customer and the product, the acceptable limits

of variation may be varied. However, some general guidelines, based on traditional Gage R & R studies, are: small variation is considered anything less than about 15%; medium variation is considered the range between 16% to 20%; large variation is considered anything over 20%. When the variation is below the 20% range, it is considered an acceptable level.

It is necessary to grasp why variation in measurement occurs in various areas of the process. The use of flow charts and cause and effect diagrams can identify critical variables. An acceptable measurement system includes determination of the quality of the system, coupled with processes for examining variation in the measurement system and the factors affecting the variation.

INSPECTION INSTRUCTIONS AS A QUALITY TOOL

A written plan is necessary to determine what to inspect for and how to do it. The planning team should include an inspector, inspector supervisor, and a quality control staff planner.

In determining the inspection stations, follow these criteria for placing the station (Juran, 1988)

- Supplier Inspection—at the movement of goods between companies
- Setup inspection—before starting a costly or irreversible operation
- Process inspection—at the movement of goods between departments
- Finished goods inspection—at the completion of the product

THE SUPPLIER'S SYSTEM QUALITY REQUIREMENTS

The quality of the product/process is no better than the components that are introduced into the production process. A supplier is expected to provide documentation confirming his actions relative to producing a quality process/product that meets the customer's needs.

It is expected that the supplier will submit to the AQP team copies of process flow chart(s), process FMEAs; and, for gray box, brown box, and black box items, a design FMEA. In addition, process control plans and statistical data pertinent to the product(s) being supplied are submitted. If the product is new to the program, program timing charts are desirable. Additional information to be requested includes the supplier's failure to meet promise dates for first piece approval programs, if any.

STATISTICAL INDEXES C_P/C_{PK}

C_p/C_{pk} indexes are a matrix form of reporting. A C_p/C_{pk} index reports the particular dimensions or process parameters and the statistical capability of the manufacturing/fabrication system to repeat itself. When viewed for an extended time period, typically in 3 month sequences covering a 6-month time period, the C_p index reveals the statistical ability of the manufacturing system to improve, remain stable, or decline with regard to statistical capability. The C_{pk} indicates the statistical capability of the manufacturing system to repeat itself when measured against the tolerance limits for the dimension or process parameter.

Each index, C_p or C_{pk}, measures a different aspect of the process/product, and each index is desirable to know. Most important, the C_p/C_{pk} index reveals long-term statistical trends. It is these long-term trends that a manager utilizes when decisions are made based on facts. Using the results of process capability studies, the following reactions are demanded:

- As a general rule in most production operations, a C_{pk} of 1.33 is the minimum acceptable level (default value). Once the process drops below this level, containment actions are expected. A typical expectation is that 100% inspection and sorting process improvements are to be made.

- With a C_{pk} above 1.33, containment action is not expected. An action plan is needed to continually improve process potential through reduction of variation.

However, remember that stability must be present before any statement of capability (C_p/C_{pk}) can be made. The following questions may help identify whether or not stability is present.

- Is there any possible over control? Is it recognized?

- Do all employees understand the importance of various indications from control charts?

- Do employees understand the time required for all sources of process variation to be represented in the data?

- Have the producer and the customer determined the period for capability evaluation?

- Are capability studies being applied only to characteristics that can be evaluated using variables data?

- For characteristics that should be evaluated with attribute data, is there an attempt being made to direct the process toward attaining stability and reducing the absolute level of concerns?

- Have the methods for calculating the standard deviation for capability evaluations been reviewed and verified as being correct?

- Are unstable and non-capable processes being given top priority for action to improve the processes?

- Have the action plans been documented for improvement?

- Is there any indication of their success in improving the processes?

- If computer-based SPC systems are in use, have the assumptions been validated as being statistically sound?

- Do the employees using the computer programs understand the output and is it being used aptly?

STATISTICAL INDEXES P_p/P_{pk}

Manufacturing process controls consist of tests and analyses that detect causes or failures during planning or production. As a consequence, these controls are based on process dominance factors, which generate significant variation. To identify the variation in relation to the target, we use the C_p or C_{pk}. As we just mentioned, however, to do that, we need data that represent long runs and/or representative runs of all situations.

In some cases, that is not possible, and, as a result, we may have to use alternative indexes. These indexes are indeed the

P_p or P_{pk}. Regardless of what index we use, it is very risky to use a process that produces an unstable product that still meets specifications. If an unstable process exists, then that process must be improved before any type of capability is performed.

Once stability is established, then one can estimate capability. For short-term samples from the process, the P_{pk} is used. Typically this measure does not include very many setups—in fact, it may only include one setup.

It must be remembered at all times that the P_{pk} is an estimate of the statistical ability to make "good" parts, that is, parts that comply with specifications. The reason is that the data used for its calculation are approximate, since they are the results of just one or two setups in a process. As a result, many long-term issues, especially special cause variation, do not appear.

Some general guidelines for a P_{pk} are:

- If the P_{pk} is greater than 1.67, then one can assume a minimum capability,

- If the P_{pk} is between 1.33 and 1.67, then one needs additional inspection steps in your process,

- If the P_{pk} is below 1.33, one must have 100% inspection to launch.

PACKAGING (PKG) TRIALS

Packaging for a product/process should allow that under normal handling, loading, and shipping conditions the products are received at a shipping destination in a damage-free condition.

Typical areas to investigate for packaging are:

- Package type—is it to be durable or expendable?

- Package classification—is it to be handled mechanically or by hand?

- Package design—does it include correct size, color, and location of package, and content identification? (Bar coding is acceptable, if it follows industry format.)

- Part protection—Is protection from rust, corrosion, distortion, breakage, contamination, shock, vibration, dimensional instability, moisture or thermal exposure, and electrostatic discharge handled appropriately?

- Is the company-owned durable containers procedure followed?

- Have alternate methods of transportation been reviewed to account for the influence of transportation mode chosen on packaging, such as: half load on truck, bad roads, vibration, and so on.

- Have warning labels for improper handling been identified and placed appropriately?

- Have all tariff provisions been accounted for?

- Have the economic disposal and recycling of packaging material been studied?

- Have the production parts and hazardous container marking identification requirements been followed?

To determine adequate packaging arrangements for the customer, contact the divisions or operations involved to determine requirements. Material handling engineers are especially helpful when determining packaging for the first time shipment of a part. After receiving an order, the AQP team begins planning for packaging as soon as it is practical.

PRE-SHIPMENT TESTING TRIAL

A trial shipment is often recommended to determine if the product is protected from normal transportation damage and other factors. All trial or test shipments are to be handled using valid sampling arrangements. An action plan is expected if there are package failures. Typical action plans should address the following:

- Trial procedures
- Condition container
- Procedure for handling packages
    Hand-handled packages
    Mechanically handled packages

- Criteria for assessing trial results
- Packaging is satisfactory and of acceptable quality: Contents of the package continue to meet the specifications and acceptable quality level. All package components arrive capable of performing their design functions.

ISR DOCUMENTATION—INITIAL SAMPLE REVIEW

The Initial Sample Review (ISR) evaluation, combined with production validation testing, confirms that the product/ process meets the customer's engineering requirements. The initial sample to be evaluated is selected from a trial production run and is submitted to layout inspection, material analysis, and specified functional tests. The functional tests include production validation testing specified in the engineering specifications and in the control plan. If the ISR demonstrates that the product/process meets all engineering requirements, the trial production run is considered a first production shipment. If the ISR and process capability studies uncover out-of-specification conditions, the inconsistencies are to be documented and a time for resolution is to be designated. Situations calling for an initial sample include:

1. new product
2. product has had a drawing, specification, or material change, or change of material source
3. product has been produced from new tools
4. product has been produced after major tooling or equipment refurbishment or rearrangement
5. product has been produced at a different manufacturing location
6. product has been produced using a new or revised process
7. product has been produced after a "stop shipment"

The product/process evaluation may be carried out at the supplier's location or samples may be submitted to the responsible purchasing division. The actual planning steps of ISR submission are:

- Determine the steps necessary for submission of the initial sample for review
- Select samples
- Prepare samples
- Determine dimensional requirements
- Determine laboratory and test requirements
- Determine engineering specifications
- Determine capability of the product/process
- Perform statistical process control
- Perform gage R & R studies
- Prepare master sample
- Submit warrant
- Achieve process flow

ISR reviews are subject to customer specifications and the necessary items are to be determined by the customer. In addition to these steps, the reader should recognize that there are five levels of submissions, with the third level as the default one. For content and sequence of the requirements see Chrysler, Ford, and General Motors (1995b).

THE PHASES AND THE APPROPRIATE ACTIONS THAT ARE EXPECTED IN EACH

As we already have mentioned, the AQP is a process. In that process many and diverse tools are used in the name of planning and improving the quality of the product, the process, or both. The phases of the AQP follow the plan-do-study-act model and are:

PLAN:
  Phase 1: Plan and define the program

DO:
  Phase 2: Design feasibility analysis
  Phase 2: Process feasibility analysis

STUDY:

Phase 3: Production planning and verification process

ACT:

Phase 4: Production part approval process (PPAP), production validation (PV), functional approval, and launch

What is interesting about these phases is the fact that each output becomes the input of the next phase. For example:

Phase 1

Inputs

Voice of the customer
  Market research
  Historical warranty and
    quality information
  Team experience
  QFDs
Business plan/marketing strategy
Product/process benchmark data
Product/process assumptions
Product reliability and
  durability studies
Customer wants and needs
  (timing and milestones)
Internal customers identified
  (which plants will assemble
  the vehicle)
Items identified for new
  technology
Preferred supply source list
Risk assessment
Custom awareness

Outputs

– Design goals determined
– Reliability and durability goals
  set
– Preliminary Bill of Material
  written
– Preliminary process flow-
  charts made
– Preliminary listing of CC/SCs
  developed
– Product assurance plan
  developed
– CFT for part, component, sup-
  plier, or sub-system identified
– Supplier program/project
  Manager assigned to CFT
– Supplier's CFT initiated
– SDS/CDS obtained
– Customs planning

The input for phase 1 is based on information from previous cross-functional team (CFT), component program management team (CPMT), and program management team (PMT) meetings; on the other hand, output are the events and activities to be completed in this phase.

Phase 2

Inputs

Customs planning
Design goals determined
Reliability and durability goals set
Preliminary Bill of Material written
Preliminary process flow charts made
Preliminary listing of CC/SCs developed
Product assurance plan developed
CFT for part, component, supplier, or sub-system identified
Supplier Program/Project Manager assigned to CFT
Supplier's CFT initiated
SDS/CDS obtained

Outputs

Design and Development
- Past failure, TGW&R, R/1000 data gathered - FMA performed
- CFTs, DFMEA, DFMA, and design reviews conducted
- Prototypes/pre-production available
- Engineering drawings, specifications, material specifications written
- Design information checklists written
- All DFMEAs completed, and all CC/SCs identified

Process Design and Development
- PFMEA conducted
- All FMEA issues addressed
- Dimensional control plans available
- Characteristics matrix developed
- Process flow chart made
- Floor plan layout designed
- Pre-launch control plan available
- New equipment, tooling, and facilities requirements and funding obtained
- Measurement systems evaluation plan developed
- Special gages/test equipment designed
- Product/process QSR conducted
- Process Instructions written
- Sub-assembly, component, or part built and tested
- SP/CP Milestones met
- Preliminary process capability study planned
- Packaging standards and specs
- Preventative maintenance schedule for process management support developed

The input for phase 2 is based on information from the outcome of phase 1, as well as previous cross-functional team (CFT), component program management team (CPMT), and program management team (PMT) meetings; on the other hand, output are the events and activities to be completed in this phase.

Phase 3

Inputs

Design and Development
Past failure, TGW&R, R/1000 data
  gathered - FMA performed
CFTs, DFMEA, DFMA, and design
  reviews conducted
Prototypes/pre-production available
Engineering drawings, specifications,
  material specifications written
Design information checklists written
All DFMEAs completed, and all
  CC/SCs identified

Process Design and Development
PFMEA conducted
All FMEA issues addressed
Dimensional control plans available
Characteristics matrix developed
Process flow chart made
Floor plan layout designed
Pre-launch control plan available
New equipment, tooling, and facilities
  requirements and funding obtained
Measurement systems evaluation
  plan developed
Special gages/test equipment designed
Product/process QSR conducted
Process instructions written
Sub-assembly, component, or part
  built and tested
SP/CP Milestones met
Preliminary process capability
  study planned
Packaging standards and specs
Preventative maintenance schedule
  for process management support
  developed

Outputs

- DFMEAs reviewed and updated
  to include all relevant
  information
- All concerns presented to
  manufacturing
- Production trial run conducted
- All DVP&Rs completed
- Measurement system evaluation
  completed
- PIST/PIPC reviewed
- Preliminary process capability
  study conducted
- Product submission warrants
  performed
- Process/production validation
  testing conducted
- Packaging evaluation completed
- Production control plan
  developed
- Quality planning signed off

The input for phase 3 is based on information from the outcome of phase 2, as well as previous cross-functional team (CFT), component program management team (CPMT), and program management team (PMT) meetings; on the other hand, output are the events and activities to be completed in this phase.

Phase 4

Inputs

DFMEAs reviewed and updated to include all relevant information

All concerns presented to manufacturing

Production trial run conducted

All DVP&Rs completed

Measurement system evaluation completed

PIST/PIPC reviewed

Preliminary process capability study conducted

Product submission warrants performed

Process/production validation testing conducted

Packaging evaluation completed

Production control plan developed

Quality planning signed off

Outputs

Ramp-up for starting date
- Conduct intensive launch efforts
- Perform dock audits with lot control/release

Production
- Long-term (run) capability studies
- Variation reduced—C_{pk} at this stage should be greater or equal to 1.33 or contained within the customer's requirements
- Customer satisfaction
- Delivery and service
- Sub-supplier reviews and audits
- Preventative maintenance program upgraded

The input for phase 4 is based on information from the outcome of phase 3, as well as previous cross-functional team (CFT), component program management team (CPMT), and program management team (PMT) meetings; on the other hand, output are the events and activities to be completed in this phase.

REFERENCE

Chrysler, Ford, and General Motors. *Measuring System Analysis.* Chrysler, Ford and General Motors. Distributed by the Automotive Industry Action Group. Southfield, MI, 1995.

Chrysler, Ford, and General Motors. *Advanced Product Quality Planning and Control Plan.* Chrysler, Ford and General Motors. Distributed by the Automotive Industry Action Group. Southfield, MI, 1995a.

Chrysler, Ford, and General Motors. *Production Part Approval Process.* Chrysler, Ford and General Motors. Distributed by the Automotive Industry Action Group. Southfield, MI, 1995b.

Juran, J.M. *Juran's Quality Control Handbook,* 4th ed. New York, NY: McGraw Hill. (1988): 13.5-13.6.

TEN

AQP Documentation and Sign-Off for Feasibility

Final acceptance of the product as being feasible is conducted prior to process review and quality planning sign-off. A final review should be conducted to determine product acceptance and conformance to engineering drawings and specifications, and meeting stipulated P_{pk} indices.

Final manufacturing feasibility indicates that a supplier is ready to deliver a proposed product/process design that can be manufactured, assembled, packaged, and shipped at a level that meets customer needs and expectations. A process review is conducted by the AQP team to confirm that all controls are in place, that the processes are being used and are in control, and that the final product/process meets engineering requirements.

QUALITY PLANNING PROCESS CHECKLIST

Control Plans

Are the plans available at all times for the affected operations?

Are the control plans posted and understood by employees?

Are the control plans being used?

Process Instructions

Are the instruction/process instruction sheets available and in use?

Are there

inspection instruction/process sheets?

laboratory test instruction/process sheets?

test procedures instruction/process sheets?

equipment operating instruction/ process sheets?

Is there proof of verification that all instruction/process sheets contain all the significant/critical characteristics found in control plans? Examples of verification are

inspection instruction/process sheets

laboratory test instruction/process sheets

test procedures instruction/process sheets

equipment operating instruction/process sheets

Have all process FMEA results been incorporated into control plans and process/instruction sheets?

Compare instruction/process sheets to control plan:

sampling plans,

process control applications,

reaction plans.

Gage and Test Equipment

Are the necessary special gages, fixtures, or test equipment available?

Are the gages, fixtures, or test equipment in use?

Are appropriate measurement system evaluation studies being conducted?

Are the results of measurements system evaluation being documented or logged?

Check Packaging

Verify that trial shipments and test methods are being conducted using proper sampling plans.

Determine corrective actions.

Determine a schedule for implementing corrective actions.

Verify corrective actions are in place.

FINAL QUALITY PLANNING SIGN-OFF

Review the sample *quality planning sign-off report* in preparation for submitting report for final acceptance before production quantities are to be shipped. At final acceptance, remember to give credit where credit is due, and *congratulate the AQP team*!

THE NEXT STEP

Pick your product and assemble the team. Remember, if your excuse is that there is no time, tomorrow is coming no matter what is decided; and it can be either an improved advanced quality system with needed competitiveness or the same old style of doing business, *chasing fires and poor planning*.

To make sure that appropriate planning and the expectation of completion of the project are realistic, make sure that the AQP team recognizes the problems of *urgency* and the importance of saying *no* where circumstances call for a *no*.

TYRANNY OF THE URGENT

In any AQP activity, it seems that we are all rushed for time because everything that we do is so important and urgent. The truth of the matter, however, is that the most important task rarely must be done today, or even this week. The urgent task calls for instant action. The momentary appeal of these tasks is irresistible and they devour our energy. But in total time perspective, their deceptive prominence fades. With a sense of loss we can recall the important tasks pushed aside. We realize we've become slaves to the tyranny of the urgent.

- A major obstacle to organizational success is allowing urgency alone to determine how resources will be consumed without considering the activity's importance to broad objectives.
- We constantly put second things first by default.
- This isn't bad—but if we get down to putting the twenty-second thing first, we are in trouble.

Check Yourself

- The last time you approached your desk to start something new, what did you select?
- Did you think through your priorities and consciously select the most important?
- Or did you allow your attention to move to:
  – the item most interesting at the moment?
  – the one your gaze happened to fall on?
  – the one brought up by a drop-in visitor?

Of course, we often do the more interesting with the rationalization that getting it out of the way will clear the decks for the more important task. Did you ever spend all day "getting organized" so you could "get to work" on the important task, only to find the time gone and nothing but inconsequentials attended to? This is a common trap, and one of the most difficult to avoid.

LEARN TO SAY NO

Perhaps the most important task for anyone involved with AQP is to challenge the priorities and schedules of due dates. We strongly recommend that the AQP team learns to say "NO!" where applicable and appropriate. Otherwise, the project deadline may fail because there were too many things to get done. Remember:

- The problem is not usually with priorities one through three, rather, it is with "posteriorities" four through infinity, as these turn out to be the "pet" projects of specific individuals with "power."

- Every project has an advocate of priority somewhere.

- Because people do not like to say no, they establish priorities and then add just a little bit of 85 other things, ending up getting nothing done.

- One simply cannot achieve excellence of performance without concentrating effort on the critical areas.

- One has to say about a suggested, but secondary project, "This is very nice, but it's not the first priority. If it must be done, we'll have to let somebody else do it."

- Keeping overall objectives in the forefront allows us to schedule time based on long-term objectives rather than immediate crisis.

- Time must not be simply consumed. It must be used wisely, so that the objectives and goals will be met.

- Learn to say no. Let somebody else do it. Do not be timid about using the greatest time-saving word in the English language, that little two-letter word "**No.**" Decide what not to do.

ELEVEN

Reliability and Maintainability

INTRODUCTION

As American automotive operations work to build more competitive products worldwide, it is important to put additional emphasis on reliability and maintainability (R & M), which support reduction of inventories and "build to schedule" targets.

For example, the *Quality System Requirements, Tooling & Equipment (TE) Supplement* to QS-9000 was developed by Chrysler, Ford, General Motors, and Riviera Die & Tool (1996) to enhance quality systems while eliminating redundant requirements, facilitating consistent terminology, and reducing costs. It is important that everyone involved in the purchase of machinery be aware of this supplement and their responsibilities as outlined in the QS-9000 process. It is also important to understand that the TE Supplement defines machinery as tooling and equipment combined. Machinery is a generic term for all hardware, including necessary operational software, which performs a manufacturing process.

The TE goal is to improve the quality, reliability, maintainability, and durability of products through appropriate and applicable planning, development, and implementation of a fundamental quality management system. The supplement communicates additional common system requirements unique to the manufacturers of tooling and equipment, as applied to the QS-9000 requirements.

WHY DO RELIABILITY AND MAINTAINABILITY (R & M)?

Due to a lack of confidence in the performance of equipment, many organizations have traditionally purchased excessive facilities and tooling in order to meet production objectives. Additionally, capital spent on "insurance-type" spare-tooling hidden for unplanned breakdowns, shows a lack of confidence in production equipment. Operational effects of production shortfalls and the inability to predict downtime are countless. These include unplanned overtime, unplanned and increasing maintenance requirements and costs, and excessive work in-process around constraint operations.

The R & M process builds confidence in predicting performance of machinery, and, through this process, we can improve the expected and demonstrated levels of machinery performance. Properly predicting and improving performance contributes to lower total cost and improved profits for the organization.

The R & M process consists of five phases that form a continuous loop. The five phases are: 1) concept; 2) design and development; 3) machinery build and installation; 4) machinery operation, continuous improvement, and performance analysis; and 5) conversion concept of next cycle. As the loop continues, each generation of machinery improves. A very cursory summary is shown in Table 24. For a detailed discussion, see Society of Automotive Engineers (1993).

In this discussion, we will concentrate on the first three phases of the loop, not because they are more important, but because they are the major focus of this effort. The last two phases are well documented in a variety of specific automotive manuals (such as FTPM—Ford total productive maintenance) and workbooks, and each automotive and/or supplier facility has a coordinator and a program moving toward the specific implementation.

Our focus then is in:

- Reliability, which is the probability that machinery and equipment can perform continuously, without failure, for a specified time (when operating under stated conditions).

- Maintainability, which is a characteristic of design, installation, and operation, usually expressed as the probability that a machine can be retained in, or restored to, specified operable conditions within a specified time interval (when maintenance is performed in accordance with prescribed procedures).

- Durability, which is the ability to perform intended function over a specified period (under normal use with specified maintenance) without significant deterioration.

Table 24. A Cursory Summary of the R & M Process

Conceptual Focus	Design & Development	Machinery Build & Installation	Operation & Support	Transition
• Confirm strategic directions, concurrent initiatives and focus • Identify critical goals, metrics and objectives • Global model of processes and information • Organize teams and assess current position • Evaluate custom regulations (if applicable) • Publish conceptual vision	• Analyze and define major functions and projects • Assess key alternative concepts • Prepare design approach, requirements, constraints, and details • Compare costs and benefits • Publish selected program (plans) & specifications	• Finalize sourcing and configuration • Prepare system • Develop systems, tests, and procedures • Integrate and test the system • Publish & start installation & monitor results • Account for safety and ergonomic regulations	• Initiate maintenance & support procedures & services • Document • Develop contingency procedures • Train personnel • Publish, support, and monitor results	• Monitor requirements and performance measures • Encourage change • Support system development • Skills transfer • Publish and support business

BASIS FOR RELIABILITY DISCUSSION

Reliability phenomena arise from the fact that a system fails to function satisfactorily during ownership, predictably, and unpredictably. Such interruptions bring pain to the user and his surroundings. Designing for reliability primarily means reducing occurrences of pain and, secondarily, providing contingencies to reduce the amount of pain in the time between the sales experience and the end of ownership.

Reliability is a measure of interruptions (known and unknown) during ownership of the product. On the other hand, reliability engineering is the science of minimizing interruptions (known and unknown) during ownership of the product. The implication is that a product will eventually fail. However, the question is when? And, if it fails, can the failure be minimized for the least effect to the user?

Reliability then, is the probability that a system will *perform* satisfactorily for a given period of time when used under stated conditions. The concept applies to any failure-prone system where failure can be addressed. Generally, after the failure is rectified, the system becomes operational.

Designing for reliability means anticipating and designing out the interruptions that may occur during the product ownership.

Improving reliability means reducing the number of known interruptions that will occur during the product ownership.

Maintainability (for failed product): Maintainability is a measure of the length of downtime due to interruptions. In a formal sense, it is the probability that a system will be restored to operational condition after failing in a specified interval of downtime when maintenance is initiated and performed as specified and without the customer feeling gouged. If failure is perceived as a repairable item, maintainability specifications must exist to design a total scenario responsive to the downtime.

Durability is not to be confused with reliability. Durability is the length of ownership. In a more formal sense, it is the probability that a system will last satisfactorily for at least a given period of time when used under stated conditions.

Availability is a combined measure of reliability and maintainability. In a formal sense, it is the probability that a system will be available for use at any point and time when operated under specified conditions.

MAKING RELIABILITY AND MAINTAINABILITY WORK

Machinery reliability and maintainability should be considered an integral part of all facilities and tooling (F & T) purchases. However, the appropriate degree of time and effort dedicated to R & M engineering must be individually applied for each unique application and purchase situation. Each project engineering manager should consider the value proposition of applying varying degrees of R & M engineering to the unique circumstances surrounding each equipment purchase.

For example, we may choose to apply a large amount of R & M engineering resources to a project that includes a large quantity of single design machines. The value proposition would show that investing up-front resources on a single design which can be leveraged beyond a single application offers a large payoff. We would also consider applying high-level R & M engineering to equipment critical to a continuous operation. On the other hand, we may choose to apply a minimal level of R & M engineering on purchase of equipment that has a mature design and minimally demonstrated field problems.

Some of the issues to consider when determining appropriate levels of R & M engineering for a project:

- Consult forecasted and available machinery and equipment (FAME) for potential machines available for reuse. FAME, as a general rule, is a specific company's web location.

- How many units are we ordering with identical or leverageable design?

- What is the condition of the existing machinery that will be rehabilitated?

- What is the status of the operating conditions? Are they extremely demanding?

- What is the cycle plan for the machinery? Does it require continuous or intermittent duty? How many years is the equipment expected to produce?

- Where is the machinery in the manufacturing process? Is it a constraint (bottleneck) operation?

- How well documented and complete is the root cause analysis for the design? Will it decrease up-front work?

- How much data exists to support known design problems?

WHO IS RESPONSIBLE?

Fully realized R & M benefits require consistent application of the process. Simultaneous engineering (SE) teams, together with the customer's plants and the supply base, must align their efforts and objectives to provide quality machinery designed for R & M. Reliability and maintainability engineering is the responsibility of everyone involved in machinery design, as much as the collection and maintenance of operational data is the responsibility of those operating and maintaining the equipment day-to-day.

The R & M process places responsibility on the groups possessing the skills or knowledge necessary to efficiently and accurately complete a given set of tasks. This is the reason the major automotive companies have realized that the expertise and knowledge are with the suppliers and, thus they are willing to delegate that responsibility to the supplier base. On the other hand, the suppliers must take the lead in the R & M efforts, if the R & M is to be successful. The R & M process encourages a company and its suppliers to lock into budget costs based on life cycle costing (LCC) analysis of options and cost targets. Warranty issues should be considered in the LCC analysis, so that design helps decrease excessive warranty costs after installation. The focus places responsibility for correcting design defects on the machinery designers.

Facility and tooling producers who practice R & M will ultimately reduce the cost (such as warranty) of their product and will become more competitive over time. Furthermore, the suppliers that do practice R & M will qualify as QS-9000-certified, preferred, global sourcing partners. Engineers and program managers that practice and encourage R & M will reduce operational costs over time. In doing so, they will meet manufacturing and cost objectives for their projects or programs.

R & M TOOLS

There are many R & M tools. The ones mentioned here are required in the design and development planning section (4.4.2) of the TE Supplement. Many others also are available to improve reliability.

- Mean time between failure (MTBF) is defined as the average time between failure occurrences. The equation would be the sum of the operating time of a machine divided by the total number of failures. For example, if a machine runs for 100 hours and breaks down four times, the MTBF would be 100 divided by four, or 25 hours. As changes are made to the machine or process, we can measure the success by comparing the new MTBF with the old MTBF and quantify the action that has been taken.

- Mean time to repair (MTTR) is defined as the average time to restore machinery or equipment to its specified conditions. This is accomplished by dividing the total repair time by the number of failures. It is important to note that the MTTR calculation is based on repairing one failure and one failure only. The length of time it takes to repair each failure directly affects up-time, up-time %, and capacity. For example, if a machine runs 100 hours and has eight failures recorded with a total repair time of 4 hours, the MTTR for this machine would be 4 hours divided by eight failures or an MTTR of .5 hours. This is the mean time it takes to repair each failure.

- Fault tree analysis (FTA) is an effect-and-cause diagram. It is used to identify the root causes of a failure mode with symbols developed in the defense industry. A benefit of FTA is the establishment of a prescriptive method for determining the root causes associated with failures. An FTA is an alternative to the Ishikawa fishbone diagram. It compliments the machinery failure mode and effects analysis (MFMEA) by representing the relationship of each root cause to other failure-mode root causes.

- Some feel the FTA is better suited to providing an understanding of the layers of and relationships among causes. An FTA also aids in establishing a troubleshooting guide for maintenance procedures.

- Life cycle costs (LCCs) are the total costs of ownership of the equipment or machinery during its operational life. A purchased system must be supported during its total life cycle. The importance of life cycle costs related to R & M is based on the fact that up to 95% of the total life cycle costs are determined during the early stages of the design and development of the equipment. The first three phases of the equipment's life cycle are typically identified as non-recurring costs. The remaining two phases are associated with the equipment's support costs.

SEQUENCE AND TIMING

The R & M process is a generic model of logically sequenced events that guides the simultaneous engineering team through the main drivers of good design for R & M engineering. The amount of time that should be budgeted for each activity or task will vary depending on the circumstances surrounding the equipment or processes in design. However, regardless of the unique conditions, all of the steps in the R & M process need to be considered in their logical sequence, and applied as needed. A typical sequence is the following:

1. Determine deadline dates to meet production requirements.

2. Check relevance of R & M activities in regards to achieving program/project targets.

3. Plan relevant R & M activities by working backwards from deadline dates, estimating time required for completion of each activity.

4. Set appropriate start dates for each activity/stage based on requirements and timing.

5. Determine and assign responsibility for stage-based deliverables.

6. Continually track progress of the plan, within and at the conclusion of each stage.

Typical activities that may take place in the first three phases of the R & M process are identified below. This list is not complete, however, it gives an idea of the type of activities that should occur during this time period. These phases are divided into main areas for consideration, then various activities are listed for each area. This list also helps identify the sequence in which these activities may be completed, depending on the project.

Concept

BOOKSHELF DATA. Activities associated with this stage are:

1. Identify good design practices.
2. Collect machinery things gone right/things gone wrong (TGR/TGW).
3. Document successful machinery R & M and FTPM features.
4. Collect similar machinery history of mean time between failures (MTBF).
5. Collect similar standardized component history of mean time between failure (MTBF).
6. Collect similar machinery history of mean time to repair (MTTR).
7. Collect similar machinery history of overall equipment effectiveness (OEE).
8. Collect similar machinery history of reliability growth.
9. Collect similar machinery history of root cause analyses.

At this point it is important to ask and respond: "Have we collected all of the relevant historical data from similar operations or designs and documented it for use during the process selection and design stages?" It is quite appropriate and effective at this stage to use surrogate data.

SURROGATE DATA DESCRIPTION. The usage of surrogate data is highly encouraged in all phases of AQP. They provide a starting point for discussion, as well as a foundation and direction for future planning. In the early stages of development, it is imperative to recognize that sometimes the appropriate and applicable data will not be available. Therefore, surrogate data is the best option, recognizing that, as direct data are accumulated, they will be used as needed. By definition then, surrogate data is the data collected on a similar part which is best in class for that commodity, either through primary or secondary sources. Surrogate data may be described as a tool for use by the process engineer (die systems and assembly) to develop a process that is: robust (functionally reliable) and cost effective, and which produces a functional part that meets customer satisfaction.

An Example of a Current Stamping Surrogate Data Process

- Conduct stamping plant engineering without assembly data. (This is a simulation scenario, at best.)
- Plant involvement.
- Lack of stamping process performance information.
- Buy off every part as unique part.
- Limited consideration given to quality performance of surrogate (no access to customer data).
- Process every part with previous model as surrogate.

Issues With Current Process

- Without customer data, optimum quality and customer value cannot be achieved.
- Excessive cost involved with:
  - Modifying dies,
  - Late tooling, and
  - Late parts for builds.
- Excessive launch costs at stamping plant.
- Inhibitor to customer's product development schedule-timing.

An Example of a Stamping Surrogate Data Pilot Process

#1	#2	#3	#4	#5	#6	#7	#8
New Model Kick-Off Meeting (At Assembly Plant)	Stamping Plant Matrixes Issues (Stamping Plant ME Manager)	Identify Surrogate Process (Die Systems)	Review Surrogate Process (Die Systems)	Develop New Stamping Process	Process Review Meetings (Process Engineer Lead)	Release New Process	Buy-off
Vehicle Line Specialist Initiates Meeting	Lessons Learned from Surrogate	Begin Review of Surrogate Data	Commence Plant Visits/ Communication		Staff Review Meeting		
Warranty Data	Quality/Yield Problems	Develop Product/Process Improvement	Gain Complete Understanding of Surrogate Process		Plant Review Meeting		
TGW Data	Dimensional Data	Request Additional Surrogate Dimensional Data From Stamping Plants if Required	Develop Best Practices Based on Surrogate Data Information		Concur on New Process List of Mandatory Attendees as per RAPID		
Control Plant Aging Matrix	Supply Matrix to Die Systems Supervisor	**Note:** The dimensional data will be Level 3 points taken at PSW. This data will be compared with Level 4 data (smaller on-going subset to compare stability and capability).					
Customer Input/Data							
Final Customer Data Includes:							
• warranty/TGW data							
• aging matrix data							
• issues in the stamping and assembly plants							
• detailed dimensional data							
Stamping Plant Input							
Assembly Plant Input							
Carry Over Part							
Quality Concerns							

Benefits of Surrogate Data Process

- Reduce die buy-off cost/timing (eliminates need to correct non-customer related issues).
- Reduce warranty.
- Improve quality by improving stamping process and considering early surrogate customer data
- Improve launches and launch cost.

Next Steps

+ Roll out process off-site

+ Hold meeting for first phase XYZ Assembly kick-off

+ Monitor selection of surrogate data; implement procedure with pilot input

+ Improve process for future implementation

MANUFACTURING PROCESS SELECTION. Activities associated with this stage are:

1. Identify general life cycle costs to drive the manufacturing process selection.
2. Establish OEE (original engineering equipment) targets including availability, quality, and performance efficiency numbers that drive the manufacturing process selection.
3. Establish broad R & M target ranges that drive the manufacturing process selection.
4. Establish manufacturing assumptions based on cycle plan, including volumes and dollar targets.
5. Identify simultaneous engineering (SE) partners for project.
6. Select manufacturing process based on demonstrated performance and expected ability to meet established targets.
7. Search FAME for surplus equipment to be considered for reuse. FAME can be accessed on the company's web site.

8. If surplus machinery has not been identified for reuse, then identify a supplier based on manufacturing process selection (evaluate R& M capability).

9. Generate detailed life cycle costing analysis on selected manufacturing process.

At this point, it is important to consider:

Have broad, high-level R & M targets been set to drive detailed process trade-off decisions?

Is the life cycle cost analysis complete for the selected manufacturing process?

Do the projections support the budget per the affordable business structure?

R & M AND TOTAL PREVENTIVE MAINTENANCE NEEDS ANALYSIS. Activities associated with this stage are:

1. Establish a clear definition of failure by using all known operating conditions and unique circumstances surrounding the process.

2. Establish R & M requirements for the unique operating conditions surrounding the chosen manufacturing process.

3. Establish/issue R & M engineering requirements for the project to the designers of the machinery.

4. Identify TPM requirements for maintainability.

At this point, it is important to consider:

Have specific R & M targets been set to support the unique operating conditions and TPM progress objectives?

DEVELOPMENT/DESIGN

R & M PLANNING. Activities associated with this stage are:

1. Conduct process concept review.

2. Identify design effects for other related equipment (automation, integration, processing, etc.).

3. Standardize fault diagnostics (controls, software, inter-faces, level of diagnosis, etc.).

4. Develop R & M/TPM plan (process/machinery FMEA, mechanical/electrical aerating, materials compatibility, thermal analyses, finite element analysis to support machine condition signature analysis, R & M predictions, R & M simulations, design for maintainability, etc.).

5. Establish R & M/TPM testing requirements (burn-in testing, voltage cycling, probability ratio sequential testing, design of experiments for process optimization, environmental stress screening, life testing, test analyze-fix, etc.).

At this point, it is important to consider:

Does the R & M plan address each project target?

Is the R & M plan sufficient to meet project targets?

PROCESS DESIGN FOR R & M. Activities associated with this stage are:

1. Conduct process design review.

2. Develop process flowchart.

3. Develop process simulation model.

4. Conduct process design simulation for multiple scenarios by analyzing operational effects of various characteristics.

5. R & M design trade-offs.

6. Develop life cycle costing analysis on process-related equipment.

7. Review process FMEA.

8. Complete final process review and simultaneous engineering team input.

At this point, it is important to consider:

Is the process FMEA complete, and have causes of potentially common failure modes been addressed and redesigned?

MACHINERY FMEA DEVELOPMENT. Activities associated with this stage are:

1. Develop plant floor computer data collection system (activity tracking, downtime, reliability growth curves).

2. Establish machinery data feedback plan (crisis maintenance, mean time between failures, mean time to repair, tool lives, overall equipment effectiveness, production report, etc.).

3. Verify completion of machinery FMEA on all critical machinery. Confirm design actions, maintenance burdens, things gone wrong, root cause analyses, etc.

4. Develop fault diagnostic strategy (built-in test equipment, rapid problem diagnosis, control measures).

5. Review equipment and material handling layouts (panels, hydro, coolant systems).

At this point, it is important to consider:

Is the machinery FMEA complete, and have causes of potentially common failure modes been addressed and redesigned?

Is the data collection plan complete?

DESIGN REVIEW. Activities associated with this stage are:

1. Conduct machinery design review (field history, machinery FMEA, test or build problems, R & M simulation & reliability predictions, maintainability, thermal/mechanical/electrical analyses, etc.).

2. Provide R & M requirements to tier 2 suppliers (levels, root cause analyses, standardized component applications, testing, etc.).

At this point, it is important to consider:

Have the R & M plan requirements been incorporated in the machinery design?

BUILD AND INSTALLATION

EQUIPMENT RUN-OFF. Activities associated with this stage are:

1. Conduct machinery run-off (root cause analysis, FRACAS, complete testing, verify R & M and TPM requirements, validate diagnostic logic and data collection).

2. Complete preventative maintenance/predictive maintenance manuals and review maintenance burden.

At this point, it is important to consider:

Has the plant maintenance devised a maintenance plan based on expected machine performance?

OPERATION OF MACHINERY. Activities associated with this stage are:

1. Implement and utilize machinery data feedback plan.

2. Implement and utilize FRACAS.

3. Evaluate TPM program.

4. Update FMEA and reliability predictions.

5. Conduct reliability growth curve development and analysis.

At this point, it is important to consider:

Have design practices been documented for use by the next generation design teams?

As the machinery begins to operate, the continuous improvement cycle phases begin to lead the R & M effort in phases 4 & 5, which are operations and support, and conversion/decommission.

OPERATIONS AND SUPPORT

After the equipment has been installed and the runoff has been performed, the durability phase of the cycle begins. The total productive maintenance (TPM) program now begins to utilize the R & M team member more as a team leader than a participant. Durability, as defined in the TE Supplement, is the "ability to perform intended function over a specified period under normal use (with specified maintenance, without significant deterioration)." As the machinery begins to acquire additional operation hours, TPM personnel identify issues and take corrective action. These issues and corrections are fed back to FMEA personnel and R & M planners as lessons learned for the next generation of machinery.

Whether these corrections are with the design of the machinery or the maintenance schedule/tasks, both must be incorporated into the continuous improvement loop.

CONVERSION/DECOMMISSION

Conversion is one of the key elements of the investment efficiency loop. The R & M process for reuse of equipment is very similar to the purchase of new equipment except that you have more limitations. The data is collected and phase 1 is repeated, often, with more specific direction as the current equipment may limit some of the other concepts.

While decommission may be the process of equipment disposal, it is necessary to verify and record R & M data from this equipment to help identify the best design practices. Also make note of the design practices that did not work as well as planned.

As plans for decommission become firm, it is important to generate forecasts for equipment availability. These forecasts should then be entered into FAME. Maintenance data, including condition, operation description, and reason for availability, should be included. This will assist engineers, evaluating surplus machinery and equipment for reuse in their program.

FAILURES

PREMATURE FAILURES. Premature failures occur due to:

- lack of understanding of the use environment
- lack of understanding of the manufacturing environment
- incompatible tolerances
- insufficient stress–strength margin

In order to reduce premature failures, the following may be used:

- Design FMEA
- Process FMEA
- Tolerance sensitivity in buildability
- Stress–strength interference

ENVIRONMENTAL FAILURES. Environmental failures occur due to:

- known environment, but not a part of design specifications
- unknown conditions
- environmental factors—ambient environment (temperature, humidity, salt, dust, rain, water, snow, wind, slopes, stones, air quality, and so on), and user environment (misapplication, abuse, user habits, and so on)

In order to reduce environmental failures, the following may be used:

- Design FMEA
- Fault Tree Analysis (FTA)
- Sneak Circuit Analysis (SCA)

WEAROUT FAILURES: Wearout failures occur due to lack of consistency and time.

In order to reduce wearout failures, the following may be used:

weak link analysis

warranty analysis

In any warranty analysis, the analyst must be aware of the following:

Common Causes	Special Causes
• Account for 85 % of warranty dollars	• Account for 15 % of warranty dollars
• Are built-in to the process	• Consist of unusual events not common across all MOPs

- Are permanent until consciously changed
- Tend to come and go, and are more locally controllable
- Are a predictable pattern of variation
- Demonstrate an instability in the pattern of variation
- Are best reduced by process improvement methodology
- Are best eliminated by a problem-solving methodology such as an 8-D

ACCELERATING QUALITY IMPROVEMENT

- Refocus our business practices, so that drivers are more systemic.

- Refocus our warranty analysis practices to be in concert with our business practices.

- Align our strategies, actions, and measures.

BREAKING THE WARRANTY ANALYSIS ADDICTION

We rely too much on find-and-fix, driven by frequent, very detailed warranty analysis. The rationale for reducing this dependency:

- We are using our customers to find our problems

- Find-and-fix is costly

- Warranty is a poor indicator for catching special causes

- Practical considerations limit the effectiveness of solutions

- Impractical approach for catching higher time in service concerns

The exception is new model launches:

- Monitor CQIS, PARSER, and SE II (see Glossary) for the first 3 to 4 months

- Examine hardware from the Warranty Parts Return Center—for trends

ESTABLISHING A NEW MINDSET

It has been said that "if you always do what you always did, you will always get what you always got." Perhaps in the past, one could "get" away with perpetuating the status quo without any major ramifications. In today's world, however, we cannot afford to blindly follow the past, since everything around us is changing. If we are committed to be "world class" in everything we do, it is imperative to change the way we do business. A fundamental change is the way we perceive the concept of globalization. Unless we recognize that globalization is not where we do business, but how we do business, we are not going to be successful. Furthermore, unless we recognize that a major concern of globalization is ultimately the business of mindset, planning, and behavior change, we are not going to get very far in the world market:

Domestic mindset to *Global mindset*

Functional expertise to *bigger picture*

Prioritize and complete action to *balance paradoxes*

Reorganize structures to *add value to processes*

Individual self-awareness to *cultural self-awareness*

Avoid surprises to *flow with change*

Demonstrate mastery to *develop life-long learning*

Some examples of the characteristics of pace-setting organizations for the world markets of yesterday and tomorrow are summarized in the following table.

Old formula for success	New formula for success
Efficiency, goal directed	Effectiveness, value-directed
Functional	Integrated, cross-functional
Hierarchical	Flatter and empowered
Geographically dependent— local, regional, national	Global

Autonomous and/or Vertically-integrated	Networked
Machine-based	Information-technology
Shareholder-focused	Stakeholder-focused
Rigid and committed	Flexible, adaptive, and learning
Product-driven	Customer-driven
Price-focused	Value-added
Product-quality focused	Total-quality focused
Efficient and stable	Innovative, entrepreneurial

It is obvious that the "old" and the "new" are quite different in many ways and the change in the thinking process in any given organization to accept the new approach may indeed be Herculean. However, no matter how one feels, change is inevitable and at least from the perspective of advanced quality planning, we recommend at a minimum, the following:

- Use warranty (and other indicators) to understand what the customer concerns are, and to prioritize them.

- Follow a process improvement approach or a new mode of operations. Use both qualitative and quantitative approaches. For example, use a QFD approach to translate the customer concerns into a specific recipe. This will involve getting answers to these questions:

  - Do we understand the customer concern?

  - Do we know how to eliminate the concern in the next design?

  - Do we know how to verify that the concern is no longer present in advance of sale to the customer?

  - If the recipe is followed, the resulting customer feedback will not be a surprise, because we have "guided the rocket, in flight, to the target." We have broken the warranty analysis addiction.

CHANGING OUR WAYS OF DOING BUSINESS

<u>Do</u>	<u>Don'ts</u>
Work on process improvement efforts aimed at correcting major systemic issues, staying with them long enough to realize progress.	React to random variation with point-to-point analyses and change directions on what to work on every month.
Identify and monitor internal company predictive metrics.	Wait for the customer to identify performance issues.
Periodically view warranty data over time at the symptom/system level to confirm expected performance levels and size up the remaining task.	Perform numerous detailed analyses, becoming hooked on looking for unexpected performance issues.
Understand the limitations of warranty—it represents customer dissatisfaction and is a significant cost burden to the company.	Think that endless analysis of warranty data will reveal root causes.

WHAT CUSTOMERS ARE LOOKING FOR

Customers, as a general rule, are interested on a good product that meets and or exceeds their requirements. To verify that their expected quality is indeed part of the product delivered, the following should be considered

> Reliability plan, which
>> address past failures experienced,
>> address potential new failures, and
>> assure, test, or inspect production and installation reliability.
> Maintainability plan, which
>> lists replacement items,

provides maintainability specs,

specifies skills required for replacing items, and

suggests administrative and logistics times involved in replacement.

Maintenance manuals, which provide

instructions including frequency, skills required, operational materials required, retest after maintenance, etc.

Operator and maintenance personnel training manuals may also be used.

Operator training is required for interface with equipment, and

maintenance personnel training is required for interface with equipment.

WHAT ARE R & M PREVENTIVE ISSUES IN DESIGN?

Machinery Suppliers

What can machinery builders foresee regarding their own equipment?

The environmental profile needs to be well understood by the machinery builders. This could include start and stop conditions, amount of space necessary/available to perform routine maintenance, handling of contingencies, etc.

Machinery builders must take into account the variability of incoming material.

Machinery builders must have reliability and maintainability goals consistent with the overall system R & M goals.

Component Suppliers

How do suppliers know and execute R & M requirements for the machinery components? Supplier of components to the system or machinery must allocate R & M goals to satisfy overall availability requirements. System integrators, machinery builders, and suppliers must coordinate to develop the list of critical components.

REFERENCE

Chrysler, Ford, and General Motors. *Quality System Requirements: Tooling & Equipment supplement.* Chrysler Corporation, Ford Motor Company, General Motors. Distributed by Automotive Industry Action Group. Southfield, MI, 1996.

Society of Automotive Engineers. *R & M Guideline for Manufacturing Machinery and Equipment.* Society of Automotive Engineers. Warrendale, PA and National Center for Manufacturing Sciences. Ann Arbor, MI, 1993.

Stamatis, D.H. *TE Supplement.* New York, NY: Quality Resources, 1998.

Chrysler Corporation's Process Sign-Off (PSO) Methodology

This appendix provides a sample of Chrysler's PSO methodology to illustrate the connection between the APQP and the PPAP. Of course, all the automotive companies have their own way of sign-off, however, we are demonstrating the significance of planning. The sign-off is the closure of all APQP, and if one has done all the work as required, when it was required, the sign-off activity becomes nothing more than a ritual, filling the forms with the appropriate authorized signatures.

A CASE STUDY OF CHRYSLER'S PSO PROCEDURE

OVERVIEW

This case study will deal with Chrysler's process sign-off (PSO) procedure. PSO is a sequential review of a supplier's manufacturing process and quality control system which is established to manage that process. The discussion will cover the evolution of PSO, the recent reorganization of

Chrysler's Procurement & Supplier Development department, and PSO as it is today.

EVOLUTION

In the early to mid 1980s, suppliers of new automotive components and/or systems were required to submit samples to Chrysler's internal receiving inspection department prior to vehicle launch. The samples were submitted with an initial sample inspection report (ISIR). The ISIR certified that the parts met specifications and were made from the production tools. Chrysler would inspect the parts; run validation tests; and ensure form, fit, function, and appearance on the vehicle.

Once approved, the supplier could be paid for the tooling of these warranted parts. In many cases, payment meant that the supplier's process was approved and the business relationship was solidified. If the supplier's process was not fully developed and capable, they would produce the parts by special 3 sigma processes or other methods and submit them for approval. Then, when it came time to produce volume, Chrysler would sometimes encounter quality and delivery problems from the incapable process.

Chrysler realized their cost of quality was high, especially appraisal costs, and made some changes to shift that cost to the supply base. In an effort to lower the cost of quality, they discontinued the receiving inspection, required the supplier to implement statistical process control (SPC), and then to become "self certified," which means capable of running their own design and process validation tests. This put the responsibility for prevention and testing on the supplier. Chrysler began performing quality audits of their suppliers in an effort to qualify and teach the suppliers the latest requirements of process control. This action was no different than that of most companies 10 years ago.

This shift to self-certification and supplier quality assurance (SQA) involvement seemed not to go as well as planned. In 1990, an effort was made to continually improve the supply base, and Chrysler implemented the priority parts quality review (PPQR). The program consisted of a 32-step AQP which combined program timing, engineering, and quality planning activities to be accomplished between the supplier and the Chrysler team. To end the program, an on-site review and PPQR sign-off was conducted at the supplier's facility. Table 25 is a sample of the milestone events as required by the AQP and PPQR sign-off (Chrysler, 1991).

Table 25. Chrysler's Milestone Events

PPQR Start (Supplier Source Selection)
Risk Assessment/feasibility issues/styling review/bill of materials
Supplier Source Approval/One-On-One
FMEA (start)
 Design (D)
 Process (P)
 Design For Manufacture and Assembly (DFMA)
Design Verification Plan & Report (DVP&R Start)
Prototype Tooling (Complete)
Phase A Pre-Production Samples and Report
Packaging R&D Review (Start)
Diamond/Shield/Pentagon Characteristic(s)
Determination/Engineering Standards Review
DV Testing, Design FMEAs (complete)
Production Release of Drawings and Engineering Standard(s)
Supplier System Plan, Control Plan, and Process FMEA (complete)
Die/Verification Model (complete)
Gages/Test Stands/Check Fixtures (complete)
Sub-Supplier Review
Gage R&R Studies
Phase B Pre-Production Samples and Report
Production Tooling (Complete)
PO Pilot Samples and Report
Preventative Maintenance Plan (Start)
Piece Production Run
 Process and Machine Capability Study (C_p, $C_{pk} > 1.33$)
PV and Reliability Testing (Complete); (Production Tooling)
DVP&R (Complete)
Sample Submission and Styling Appearance Review
PTR (Production Trial Run)
Outer Drive Pilot Review
Packaging Final Approval
C1 Pilot
PVP
Piece FPSC Program
 Process Capability (C_p, $C_{pk} > 1.33$)
PPQR Sign-Off/On-Site Review (complete)
V1 Launch
Note: All italicized items are considered to be master timing schedule (MTS) dates.

The combination of Chrysler's AQP and PPQR program plus the Automotive Industry Action Group (AIAG) publications, namely PPAP and QS-9000, are responsible for the foundation and development of the PSO. The latest version of the PSO blue dot manual was published January 23, 1996, after going through revisions in the fall of 1995.

PROCUREMENT AND SUPPLY REORGANIZATION

Chrysler Corporation's supplier quality function is known as supplier development and is managed by the Procurement and Supply Department. Until recently, the supplier quality specialists were platform-based and handled quality planning activities by the vehicle rather than the commodity. This meant that each specialist had responsibility for various components and systems within the vehicle. For example, one specialist on the Plymouth Prowler was responsible for AQP airbags, wiring, exterior lighting, and engine cooling. The supply base had difficulty in maintaining continuity among the specialists, because of the diversity of the specialists and the number of different vehicles Chrysler produced. Another problem with platform quality was the breadth of knowledge required across various systems and components. On March 4, 1996, Chrysler reorganized by commodity rather than platform.

This reorganization affected the entire Procurement and Supply Department including Purchasing and Supplier Development. Chrysler was reacting to J.D. Powers' survey which indicated that Chrysler had poor quality compared with its competitors. Chrysler felt the new commodity-based organization would lend continuity to the supply base, promote team effort between the buying community and SQA in terms of both quality and cost savings, and, perhaps most importantly, allow the SQA specialists to become experts in their specific commodities.

The buying community was affected as well because a number of buyers were blended, i.e., the buyer was also responsible for supplier quality, PSO, and commercial issues. The buyers are now deblended and responsible for commercial issues.

PROCESS SIGN-OFF

Process sign-off (PSO) is a 21-point review of the supplier's manufacturing process for a given automotive component or process. The review covers the entire production system, as well the engineering, quality planning, and testing that went into the development of the process and/or component. Included in the review are manpower, facilities, equipment, materials, methods, procedures, software, and tooling.

PSO applies to any new, modified, or carry-over component which has a high or medium risk assessment. It is mandatory on any new high risk component. Chrysler has developed a 33-page blue dot manual titled *Process Sign-Off (PSO)*. (The latest revision is January 23, 1996 and can be ordered under publication number 84-231-1227 from Proforms Incorporated at 313-513-3676.)

There are three working papers that are used when conducting PSO. Their essence is summarized in a 21-point checklist (Chrysler, "process...," 1996). Each item must be reviewed with the supplier by the product team. The 21 items (elements) of the checklist are identified in Table 26. For additional explanation, review Chrysler's PSO manual, under *Guidelines*.

Table 26. Process Sign-Off Checklist of 21 Points

1. Part number description and change level
2. Process flow diagram and manufacturing floor plan
3. Design FMEA and process FMEA
4. Control plan
5. Incoming and outgoing material qualification certification plan
6. Evidence of product specifications
7. Tooling, equipment, and gages identified
8. Significant product and process characteristics identified
9. Process monitoring and operating instructions
10. Test sample sizes and frequencies
11. Parts handling plan
12. Parts packaging and shipping specifications
13. Product assurance plan (PAP)
14. Engineering standards identified
15. Preventive maintenance plans
16. Gage and test equipment evaluation
17. Problem-solving methods
18. Production validation complete
19. BSR / NUV
20. Line speed demonstration and capability evaluation
21. Error- and mistake-proofing

This checklist is the main document that controls the sign-off for PSO. Also, this checklist requires the following information to be recorded: approvals by both Chrysler and supplier PSO team, supplier and part information, appropriate and applicable dates, corrective action, on site revisit, and signatures.

The heart of the form is the 21 topics for documentation and process accept/unaccept findings box. The Chrysler quality specialist leads the team and completes the checklist based on the team's findings. Corrective actions should be documented on the supplemental follow-up comments page.

The purpose of PSO is to verify the supplier's production readiness and capability. This is by done by witnessing the production operation, function at the quoted daily line rate, following all of the procedures developed to control the process. The process must prove capability and be able to produce with a P_{pk} of 1.67 or greater.

PSO is conducted at the supplier's plant or second-tier plant by the product team from Chrysler and the supplier as follows.

Chrysler   **Supplier**

Engineering   Quality Assurance Manager

Supplier Quality   Manufacturing Manager

Supplier Management   Plant Manager

The supplier is ready to conduct PSO when all documentation from the 21-point checklist is completed and approved. All production tooling used to produce the product must be complete and set up in the manufacturing line. The operators must be trained and provided with written work instructions, complete with samples and/or visual aids.

Finally, the product/process is ready when trial runs to assess tool performance, trouble shoot the process, and run preliminary capability studies are finished. The initiation of PSO should commence after the F1 program vehicles are built and before P0 pilot parts are built, approximately 60 weeks before volume launch. This time frame puts the beginning of PSO in the middle of the vehicle's development. Completion of the PSO process should be targeted for P0 pilot, no later than C1 pilot, with fully approved parts submitted under the Production Part Approval Process (PPAP) (Chrysler, Ford and General Motors, 1995).

To understand Chrysler's product development process in detail, the reader is encouraged to see (Chrysler, "Process...," 1996). To be sure, Chrysler uses simultaneous engineering in the development process of the vehicle. In fact, there are many cross-functional teams working together, performing such activities as quality planning, design engineering, and conducting validation tests for both product and process development for the manufacture of components and the vehicle assembly process. These cross-functional teams are known as AQP Teams and are responsible for keeping the planning development and timing on track.

How is the team been kept on track? The quality specialist plans a minimum of three meetings which encompass an eight-step strategy which will be discussed later. The three meetings are as follows: 1) Pre-plant visit meeting (strategy steps 1-3), which is the formal start of the procedure. Prior to the plant visit, the product team will review the supplier's documentation against the elements to be audited on the 21-point PSO checklist. The team is to determine whether the supplier is ready to perform the production demonstration run. 2) PSO plant visit (strategy step 4 and 5), to witness the demonstration run. 3) PSO sign-off completion (strategy steps 6-8), to review production validation tests, open issues from the 21-point checklist, and submit the PPAP warrant.

THE PROCESS SIGN-OFF STRATEGY

The process sign-off strategy consists of eight steps, as follows:

1. Review PSO requirements with the team and supplier.

   PSO is an ongoing quality planning activity that normally takes place during the vehicles development by the AQP team for high-risk parts. Medium to low risk parts may not require the weekly and bi-weekly team meetings that high-risk components do. Therefore, a separate meeting would be called by the supplier quality specialist prior to P0 pilot build, to ensure that the engineer and the supplier know the requirements of PSO.

2. Review the supplier's documentation.

The suppliers are required to provide documentation supporting the 21-point checklist. The documentation should be supplied in a binder. If accepted, these quality documents will become the standard against which the product/process will be evaluated by the product team, during the production demonstration run. All documentation checklist points should be marked acceptable with the exception of number 18, production validation (PV) tests. The PV test parts are to come from the upcoming production demonstration run. At this stage, the design validation and production plan and report should not be complete. However, the PV test plan should be determined and available.

3. Conduct pre-plant visit meeting.

The purpose of this meeting is to set the agenda for plant visit and demonstration run. The team should verify that the checklist is approved and in order. Review the characteristic to be measured during the demonstration. Go over again the flow charts, control plan, quantity and line rate to be produced. Finally, review the requirements and timing of the First Production Shipment Certification (FPSC) program.

4. Conduct plant visit.

The plant visit is actually combined with step #5. It represents the transition from the documentation ("tell me") phase to the beginning of the process ("show me") phase. The purpose is to witness the production, verify the preliminary results, and audit the procedures. Proper etiquette requires an entrance and exit interview with plant management to explain the purpose, agenda, and results of the visit.

5. Perform production demonstration run.

   This step is the actual on-floor validation run of the process. The team must witness the manufacture of the components at rate, utilizing the actual production equipment with production tools. A minimum of 300 parts or 2 hours of production should be run, whichever is greater. The team must also witness gaging to determine process capability, which should be at least 1.67 P_{pk} for each characteristic.

6. Conduct process validation (PV) test.

   Components from the production demonstration should be submitted and tested per the PV test plan. This should include laboratory tests, in-vehicle assembly, and tests.

7. Complete process sign-off.

   Review PV test results with the product team. Check for any open corrective actions. All 21 points on the checklist should be marked acceptable for documentation as well as process. It is made clear to the supplier that the process cannot be changed without written approval and/or revalidation from Chrysler.

8. Submit PPAP warrant.

   At the time of sign-off, the PPAP warrant should be filled out with supporting documentation depending on the level of submission required. This submission should be in time for the C-1 pilot. If PSO has not been completed then, an Interim Approval Authorization (IAA), approved by the program executive, will be required to accompany the components for the C-1 vehicle build.

   Submittal of the approved PPAP warrant and PSO checklist completes the development process. After the PSO, the supplier must continue to build components as specified under the PSO. Any changes must be approved by Chrysler and SQA.

REFERENCE

Chrysler Motor Company. *Process Sign-Off.* Auburn Hills, MI: Supplier Development, 1996.

Chrysler Motor Company. *Priority Parts Quality Review Program Procedure: PPQR.* Auburn Hills, MI: Supplier Quality, 1991.

Chrysler, Ford and General Motors. *Production Part Approval Process: PPAP.* Chrysler, Ford and General Motors. Distributed by Automotive Industry Action Group (AIAG). Southfield, MI, 1995.

How to Interpret Warranty Data

To optimize the results of AQP using warranty data, we must recognize that point-to-point comparisons are not effective for analysis. This is because they show only special causes and not the true reason for any long-term problems. Second, we must recognize that warranty data can provide information that shows the real causes of problems. If we study the following:

- Common versus special causes
  - Look for inherent versus assignable (special) causes
- Interpreting run charts
  - Look for predictable versus unusual patterns
- Process shifts
  - Look for shifts of the average
  - Look for percentage points of the normal distribution
  - Look for shifts in the run chart
  - Look for patterns and shifts over time
- Run rules
  - Look for the specific rules that indicate the process is out of control, given a set of data on the chart

Strategic Approach to Warranty

Even though warranty analysis is an appraisal system, it can and, in fact, does provide valuable information for future and current design, process, and service improvements. It does that by utilizing the information as a feedback loop to the system and by applying the following strategies:

- Accelerate quality improvement
- Revise the management by objective system
- Develop a management by objective system to reflect attainable goals within realistic time constraints
- Break the warranty analysis addiction
- Group warranty data
- Look for trends in warranty data
- Use a problem-solving methodology to identify, analyze, and evaluate data
- Never use point-to-point comparisons

Sample Business Plan

This appendix contains a sample business plan (without any appendices or schedule of capital expenditures) to demonstrate that a business plan not only is a requirement for all APQP endeavors (see AIAG publication on *Advanced Product Quality Planning*), but also provides the framework for the quality plan in any organization.

Quite often, a business plan may define parameters of operation and place constraints on timing, cost, and other resources. As a consequence, the AQP team should be familiar with the contents of a business plan.

BUSINESS PLAN FOR DOWNTOWN ELECTRO-COATING

Prepared:_____ Date: _____ Authorized:_____ Date: _____

TABLE OF CONTENTS

Executive summary

Background

Goals and objectives

Marketplace

Competition

Marketing plan

Operations

Business expansion

Quality assurance

Human relations

Financial

Assumptions to the financial projections

Appendix (in this sample no appendices are included)

EXECUTIVE SUMMARY

BACKGROUND

Downtown E-Coatings Company was established as a limited liability company (L.L.C.) in April 1996, and began formal operation as a separate company in August 1996. The company purchased the E-coat operations of ABC Automotive Manufacturing Company.

In 1983, Aristidis and Nikolaos Philis formed ABC Automotive Manufacturing Company as a Detroit-based automotive stamping plant. This plant specialized in producing large automotive stampings such as hoods, door panels, quarter panels, bumpers, and similar parts for General Motors, Ford, and Chrysler. At its peak, the company had contracts in excess of $30 million, but was severely impacted by the OEM automotive companies' shrinking of their supply base. Today, the stamping operations are a Tier II and Tier III supplier of stamped parts and welded assemblies.

The coating business grew, and, in 1986, the company upgraded to the latest in coating technology, electro deposition coating or, as it is commonly known, E-coating. Our system has been continually upgraded to keep pace with technical developments and continues to be "state of the art." We are capable of painting the widest array of parts in the industry, from very small parts to very large parts, such as body panels. This is in contrast to the majority of our competitors, who are limited to small parts.

We are actively pursuing new E-coat business with a target of production schedules to operate on a full three-shift operation. Concurrently, we plan to invest in our business by a "Class A" powder coat finishing system that complements our current prime coat system.

KEY EMPLOYEES

Aristidis Philis is a Member of the L.L.C. and the Chief Executive of Downtown E-Coatings.

Nikolaos Philis is a Member of the L.L.C. and a Senior Company Executive.

George Kolias is the General Manager of Downtown E-Coatings.

OWNERSHIP

Downtown E-Coatings (DEC) company is a limited liability company (L.L.C.). Its members are Aristidis and Nikolaos Philis.

GOALS AND OBJECTIVES

Downtown E-Coatings will be managed in such a manner as to profitably optimize our growth while providing "world class" quality products and services to our customers and utilizing all of our assets. To meet these goals, we will pursue the following objectives.

1. Increase E-coating sales by a minimum of 15% and decrease packaging incidents by 8%.
2. Develop control systems to reduce quality problems and improve delivery time to customers by 15%.

3. Reduce cost as a percentage of revenue by a minimum of 5% through improved efficiency and implementation of new control systems.

4. Obtain QS-9000 certification.

5. Work towards ISO 14000 certification.

6. Substantially expand our business by adding a "state of the art" powder coat finishing system.

7. Integrate the remaining stamping operations into Downtown E-Coatings, and,

8. Actively participate in the renaissance of the Empowerment Zone.

MARKETPLACE

The Michigan area is the largest market for the use of E-coating prime coat painting in the world. While all body panels, framing, and suspension are E-coated in the OEMs' own facilities, supplied components and most service parts are coated at outside facilities. This represents a significant business opportunity for our company. While there is a wide array of competitors offering this service, very few can coat parts as large as DEC can.

COMPETITION

DEC markets primarily in the XYZ metropolitan area of the South section of Michigan and the North section of Ohio. We are constantly facing new competitors entering our business market, competing for the same customers. Because of this, our commitment to quality has been forged to include a commitment of leadership in the industry. One of our main objectives is to become the "benchmark company," by which both our customers and our competitors judge performance. To reach that objective, we are constantly reviewing our competitors' strengths and weaknesses, as well as the leaders in our technology.

MARKETING PLAN

POSITIONING. DEC has positioned itself as a niche marketer of prime coatings and packaging for both the OEM automotive manufacturers' service parts operations and for a variety of Tier II and aftermarket companies.

STRATEGIES. Additional sales are critical to the continued success of DEC and must be pursued aggressively. Improved performance with our current customers offers the best opportunity for additional business. Pursuing new customers will occur at the same time.

To support these strategies and our company goals, we plan to meet these marketing objectives by:

1. Pursuing both current and new customers to increase E-coat sales by a minimum of 15% and packaging by a like amount during 1998.

2. Developing our inside sales organization to fully support our customers in technical issues.

3. Adding additional independent sales representatives and outside salesmen to support this effort.

4. Utilizing our Empowerment Zone location to help penetrate large automotive customers.

5. Establishing partnering relationships with our customers to obtain more of their business.

6. Marketing finish coating services aggressively when we are in a position to add this system to our facility, and,

7. Developing and implementing a program for marketing warehousing space.

OPERATIONS

We have substantial experience within our company in all areas of painting, finish packaging, stamping, welding, and assembly. We will utilize that experience to improve the efficiency of our operations and provide a level of service that will be the "benchmark" for our industry. To implement this direction and support our company's goals, we will meet or exceed the following objectives by the following actions.

1. Implement systems that will allow us to adequately track and control our process to "best in class" levels.

2. Improve the production control process to assure that all material being processed through our plant meets or exceeds customer timing and shipping requirements.

3. Reduce manufacturing cost by a minimum of 5% in current operations through improved efficiency and implementation of control systems.

4. Provide necessary training to allow all employees to perform their jobs to specification.

5. Provide all necessary support to the achievement of QS-9000.

6. Maximize efficiency by cross-training workers to improve their skills and provide the company with improved flexibility.

7. Utilize our trucking service to provide a cost beneficial support service for our customers.

8. Reduce in-plant quality problems by a minimum of 15% during 1998.

9. Integrate the remaining stamping operations into the DEC system.

10. Repair, clean, and segment the warehouse for leasing.

11. Plan, lay out, and bring on line a new powder coat finish paint facility to expand our business.

QUALITY ASSURANCE

Quality is the bedrock upon which our company will continue to grow and prosper. DEC's operating philosophy is to meet or exceed our customers' requirements on every part we produce. We plan to be the "benchmark leaders" against which our competitors measure their own performance. To support this and other company goals, we plan to meet or exceed the following objectives.

1. Continue to involve all employees in the process of meeting or exceeding the customers' requirements.

2. Provide all employees with the necessary training to make a meaningful contribution to our quality standards and overall performance.

3. Develop and implement the systems and processes necessary to obtain QS-9000 Certification in early 1988, and ISO 14000 certification be the end of 1999.

4. Control all incoming material throughout our internal processes.

5. Develop systems to capture and make available to management the cost of non-conformance,.

6. Vigorously pursue continual improvement.

HUMAN RELATIONS

Our employees are our most valuable assets. We provide a safe and clean environment that allows our employees to perform their jobs to the best of their abilities. To support the company's goals, we will pursue the following objectives:

1. Continue to improve communication throughout the company.

2. Provide a training matrix for all of our employees.

3. Provide functional cross-training to improve employees' skills and company flexibility.

4. Continue to improve the relationship with our union by administering the contract in a cooperative and a fair approach.

FINANCIAL

As with any successful company, DEC projects its financial results as a consequence of the actions anticipated in its business plan. To assist in achieving these results, we plan to:

improve our cost tracking and control systems and

closely monitor our results and compare them to our business plan.

As a result of the actions planned, we expect 1998 sales to be in the $8.0 million range, and to rise substantially to $20.2 million by 2001. Operating profit is expected to increase from $347,000 in 1997 to $2.8 million in 2001.

BACKGROUND

Downtown Electro-Coatings (DEC) Company L.L.C. began operation August 1996. The company was formerly the E-Coat Operation of ABC Automotive Manufacturing Corporation.

In 1983, father and son, Aristidis and Nikolaos Philis, formed ABC Automotive Manufacturing Company as a Detroit-based automotive stamping plant, manufacturing large sheet metal parts. Stamped parts include hoods, door panels, quarter panels, bumpers, frame rails, cross members, and wheel wells. By the third year of operation, ABC had secured over $30 million in contracts, principally from General Motors, Ford Motor Company, and Chrysler Corporation. In the late 1980s and early 1990s, as the domestic automotive companies readjusted their supply base, ABC lost a significant portion of their business and today is a Tier II or Tier III supplier of stamped parts.

Painting business remained strong and, in 1986, the company upgraded from a flow-coat system to the current E-coat system. This system has been continually upgraded and is "state of the art" for electro-coating. We are capable of painting a full range of parts from small miscellaneous parts to large parts, such as body panels. The majority of our competitors cannot paint these large parts.

We plan to continue to invest in DEC and to expand our business by adding a "Class A" finishing system. This will be accomplished by adding a complete powder coat finish system, capable of finishing parts as large as our current E-coat system.

To further focus our efforts in expanding our coating business, the stamping business has been reduced to two stamping lines with supporting welding and assembly, to supply our current manufacturing business and to support coatings. This reduced operation has been absorbed into DEC. All of the remaining equipment is in the process of being sold to reduce debt.

KEY EMPLOYEES

Aristidis Philis is a member of the L.L.C. and the Chief Executive of DEC. In his position, he provides future direction and strategies for the company. He also monitors the performance of the senior company managers. A biography on Aristidis Philis is included in Appendix A of this plan.

Nikolaos Philis is a member of the L.L.C. and a Senior Company Executive. In his position, he provides guidance and direction to senior company executives and directs special projects, with focus on leading technology applications. A biography on Nikolaos Philis is included in Appendix A.

George Kollias is the General Manger. In his position he provides operational direction for the company and manages the activities of all of the company's operations. A biography on George Kollias is included in Appendix A.

OWNERSHIP

Downtown Electro-Coating is a Limited Liability Company (L.L.C.). Its members are Aristidis and Nikolaos Philis.

GOALS AND OBJECTIVES

DEC, L.L.C. will be managed in such a manner as to profitably optimize the growth, while providing "world class" quality products and services to our customers and utilizing all of our assets. We will build upon our position as a provider of prime coat painting and finish packaging to expand into powder coat finish coating. To meet these goals, we will pursue the following objectives.

1. Increase E-coating sales by a minimum of 15% and decrease packaging incidents by 8%.

2. Develop control systems to reduce quality problems, and improve delivery to customers by 15%.

3. Reduce cost as a percentage of revenue by a minimum of 5% through improved efficiency and implementation of new control systems.

4. Obtain QS-9000/ISO 9002 certification.

5. Work towards ISO 14000 certification.

6. Substantially expand our business by adding a "state of the art" powder coat finishing system.

7. Integrate the remaining stamping operations into Downtown E-coatings.

8. Actively participate in the renaissance of the Empowerment Zone.

MARKETPLACE

The XYZ area is the single largest market for the use of Electro-coating prime coat painting in the world. All major body panels, suspension, and framing on all automotive vehicles are Electro-coat prime coated. In addition, significant portions of all associated metal parts are also Electro-coated. While most primary production body, suspension, and frame parts are coated at the automotive assembly facilities, supplied components and most service parts are coated at outside facilities. This represents a significant business opportunity for companies supplying Electro-coat prime painting.

There is an array of suppliers of this service to this market. They range from large stampers with their own coating facilities to small, specialized manufacturers who outsource all coatings. Of the large coating manufacturers, few offer all coating options—plating, Electro-coat prime coating, and "Class A" finish coating. The majority of Electro-coat prime paint suppliers have systems that can only handle small parts. There are very few that can handle large parts such as hoods, fenders, and quarter panels.

COMPETITION

DEC markets primarily in the XYZ metropolitan area, the south section of Michigan and the north section of Ohio. We are constantly facing new competitors trying to enter our business market, competing for the same customers. Because of this, our commitment to quality has been forged to include a commitment of leadership in the industry. One of our main objectives is to become the "benchmark company," by which both our customers and our competitors judge performance. To reach that objective, we are constantly reviewing our competitors' strengths and weaknesses, as well as the leaders in our technology.

The main competitors of Downtown Electro-Coatings and some of their strengths and weaknesses are as follows.

Company	Strength	Weaknesses
A	Certified minority supplier Competitive pricing Good GM relationship	Poor location Low employee skill base No large part capability
B	Low pricing Recent added capacity (Good Budd Co.) relationship	Fair product quality Difficult to deal with customers No large part capability
C	Excellent scheduling Aggressive transportation	Poor location No large part capability 24-hour minimum turnaround
D	Very low pricing	Small parts only capability Very dirty environment
E	Good quality Large to small parts	High price Poor location

MARKETING PLAN

POSITIONING

DEC Company has positioned itself as a niche company of prime coatings and packaging for both the OEM automotive manufacturers' service parts operations and for a variety of Tier 2 and aftermarket companies. This niche provides the opportunity for future growth in both prime coating and finish coating as the company expands.

STRATEGIES

Additional sales are critical to the continued success of DEC. Opportunities abound in the markets currently serviced by the company and must be pursued aggressively. Improved performance with our current customers will serve as an incentive for additional business and a strong base from which to obtain new customers. In a separate but concurrent action, we will develop and implement a plan to market warehouse space in our 360,000 square foot warehouse.

To support the company goals, we plan to meet these marketing objectives by:

1. Pursuing both current and new customers to increase E-coat sales by a minimum of 15% and packaging by a like amount during 1998.

2. Developing our inside sales organization to fully support our customers in technical issues.

3. Adding additional independent sales representatives and outside salesmen to support this effort.

4. Utilizing our Empowerment Zone location to help penetrate large automotive customers.

5. Establishing partnering relationships with our customers to obtain more of their business.

6. Marketing finish coating services aggressively when we are in a position to add this system to our facility.

7. Developing and implementing a program for marketing warehousing space.

CURRENT CUSTOMERS

The current customers are the base for further expansion and represent the largest potential for new business. It is our plan to establish a partnering relationship with key customers as a vehicle for obtaining a greater portion of their coating business. We will substantially improve our service to these customers. We are training an inside sales person who will always be available to follow up on customer inquiries and to contact customers for information we require to properly service their needs. We are also targeting improvements on turnaround and in control of customer's parts when they are in our process. In addition, we will offer other incentives, such as warehousing of parts, packaging, subassembly, and other extended processes.

NEW CUSTOMERS

Our ability to obtain new customers will relate directly to our rate of growth. We have undertaken an aggressive program to identify and target new customers. This is a joint effort among DEC sales, marketing, the current sales representative, new sales representatives, and company management. We have added additional internal support for our Sales Manager to allow him to spend more time visiting customers and prospects. Our inside sales person will be available to follow up customer inquiries and our Manager of Administration will be able to quote parts and to set up new parts for the system. In addition, we will add an additional company sales representative in the first quarter of 1998.

We have provided additional incentives for our current independent representatives to aggressively pursue new business. We will work with them and provide any additional support they need, such as plant visits, sales and marketing support, and technical help.

To expand our sales capability, we are actively pursuing additional sales representatives to sell Electro-coating services. Currently we are using word of mouth and contacts possessed by members of our management team to pursue this goal. We plan to expand this search by advertising in selected industry journals. It is our objective to add three new representatives in 1998.

EMPOWERMENT ZONE

We are aggressively promoting our location in the Empowerment Zone to sell our capabilities to both the OEM automotive manufacturers and to their large Tier 1 suppliers. These companies have committed to move additional business to companies in the zone and we are prepared to take full advantage of this commitment.

CROSS MARKETING

DEC has the ability to offer customers painting, packaging, and warehousing. In addition, it has the capability to offer warehousing and shipping from a consigned inventory directly to our customers' customers. Furthermore, with its own trucks, it can, if planned properly, pick up from and deliver product to customers in a reasonable geographic area. We plan to market these services to both current and new customers as added incentive for new business.

WAREHOUSE MARKETING

Our current standalone warehouse has 360,000 square feet of storage space. This is far in excess of what is required for our own use. The cost of this facility is currently a drain on the other business and must be relieved.

Our strategy is to develop and implement a marketing plan to lease out the unused space in this building. We are working with specialists in this type of leasing to achieve our goal. We are currently in the process of repairing the roof and cleaning and lighting the newly dry areas. We plan to continue our refurbishing process as funds are available and the weather conducive to repairs. Over time, the entire structure will be repaired and leased as warehouse or light manufacturing space.

STAMPING AND ASSEMBLY

XYZ Automotive Stamping has seen substantially reduced operations in the past few years. A decision has been made to close that company, sell off portions of the equipment, and transfer selected equipment and the current customers to DEC.

We plan to continue to serve our current stamping and assembly customers, primarily WS Co., UV Specialty Stamping, Quality Craft, and Progressive Stamping. We will then seek additional business in both stamping and assembly that fits our new capabilities. Our current sales and marketing organization and the independent representatives will also service this market.

POWDER COATING

A logical extension of our current prime coat services is to provide finish coating. This would allow many of our customers and target customers to deal with a single source for both their prime and finish coating needs. Powder coat finish coating is one major area of growth. This coating provides a very durable finish with "Class A" capability and substantial environmental advantages since it does not release volatile solvents to the atmosphere as part of the process.

We have identified light truck bumpers, frame cross members, trailer hitches, "Class A" body panels, bumper reinforcement bars, stabilizer bars, coil springs, wheels, sun roofs, engine mounts, and similar parts as prime candidates for our new system. We are talking to both our current customers and to targeted prospects that manufacture these parts about their interest in our supplying this service. Initial interest is good and we will continue to pursue additional potential business. Assuming that we will identify enough business to justify our entry, we will develop and build a "state of the art" powder coat facility that will provide "Class A" finishes for as wide an array of parts as our E-coat system is capable of. This will allow us to market ourselves as a full service coating business.

OPERATIONS

We have substantial experience within our organization in all areas of painting and finish packaging. We will utilize that experience to improve the efficiency of our operations and provide a level of service to our customers that will be the "benchmark" for our industry. To implement this direction and to support the company's goals, we will meet or exceed these objectives by taking the following actions:

1. Implementing systems that will allow us to adequately track and control our processes to "best in class" levels.

2. Improving the production control process to ensure that all material being processed through our plant meets or exceeds customer timing and shipping requirements.

3. Reducing manufacturing cost by a minimum of 5% in current operations through improved efficiency, and implementing of control systems.

4. Providing necessary training to allow all employees to perform their jobs to specification.

5. Providing all necessary support to achieve QS-9000 certification.

6. Maximizing efficiency by cross-training workers to improve their skills and provide the company with more flexibility.

7. Utilizing our trucking service to provide a cost-beneficial support service for our customers.

8. Reducing in plant quality problems by a minimum of 15% during 1998.

9. Integrating the remaining stamping operations into the DEC system.

10. Repairing, cleaning, and segmenting the warehouse for leasing.

11. Planning, laying out, and developing the sight to bring on line a new powder coat finish paint facility to expand our business.

PRODUCTION CONTROL

Our primary business is the coating of our customers' parts. To meet their specifications for quantity, handling, packaging, and delivery requires a control system that assures compliance. Our primary vehicle to achieve this will be a lot control system that tracks all parts from receiving through our process to shipping. This system will allow us to monitor our progress against the customer's timing requirements and assure that what was received was shipped after processing. The initial system will be manual, progressing to computer-assisted and finally to bar-coding. We are in the process of developing and implementing this system. All personnel involved in the receiving, processing, and shipping of material will be given the required training.

An improved scheduling system is also in the development process. We currently schedule and closely monitor all small parts being processed. Our next step is to formally schedule large parts in the same manner as small parts.

Finally, we have strengthened this function with the addition of an experienced manager and provided additional training for the other members of the department.

MATERIAL CONTROL AND PURCHASING

DEC also provides packaging services to supplement our coatings business. This packaging must be available when required to ship the customer's product. The careful planning and management of the packaging inventory represents a significant area for both strong support of our coatings business and substantial savings in our purchases.

We are also pursuing partnering with our suppliers as well as our customers. Our commitment to Abe Chemical Co. for our paint has resulted in a switch from frequent small purchases to the installation of a 7,800-gallon tank, funded by our supplier, which allows them to supply us in bulk and us to enjoy the price reduction from bulk purchasing. We plan to pursue blanket purchases with our packaging and other suppliers to obtain further cost savings.

PROCESS CONTROL

To ensure that all of our processes meet specification, each part is accompanied by a Part Processing Information Sheet (PPIS) when it is transported to the hanging areas. This sheet provides all of the information required to properly process the part—a picture of how the part is hung, the paint specification, and the instructions for packaging. Each employee is trained to refer to this sheet before he/she starts the job and not to hang any part that does not have one of these sheets. These instructions are reinforced at meetings held before each shift.

TRAINING

Training is a critical element of continual improvement. We plan to provide additional training for all of our people to improve their skills. Our manufacturing supervision will receive formal supervisor training. Their improved skills will allow them to be a catalyst for the other employees. Cross-functional training will allow the company more flexibility and improve efficiency. The detailed training plan is included in Appendix B of this plan.

QUALITY IMPROVEMENT

As we implement our improvements in monitoring and control systems and employees improve their skills through training, we expect to continually improve upon our already high level of quality. We have begun tracking the cost of quality and communicating the results to our employees. DEC will provide support and the necessary tools for this effort as well as recognition for their success.

TRUCKING

DEC has two tractors, several trailers, and a box truck. These provide us with the opportunity for a competitive advantage. We will maximize this advantage through careful scheduling and efficient use of this asset in obtaining new business with both current and new customers.

WAREHOUSE REPAIR

We are developing and implementing a plan to repair the roof, clean, segment, and wall off sections of the warehouse. As each section is successfully completed, we will begin to actively market it to prospective customers. We will use our own employees for as much of this work as is practical and only contract for outside specialists where necessary. As revenue is generated, we will fund additional repairs and cleanup, and increase the portion of the building available until the entire building is repaired and leased out.

ENVIRONMENTAL CONSIDERATIONS

We closely monitor all of our systems to ensure compliance with environmental requirements. As a good corporate citizen, we try to improve upon the assets we utilize. One of our improvements is the substitute of non-chrome finishing for chrome in our pre- and post-finishing system. This allows us to reduce treatment of our effluents while providing an environmentally friendly system. This is accomplished while still meeting customers' requirements. Our wastewater treatment system returns water to the system in cleaner condition than when it was received.

Our long-term goals in the environmental domain include an ISO 14000 certification by the end of 1999.

BUSINESS EXPANSION

POWDER COATING

We plan to expand our capabilities into powder coat finish coating. This will entail the purchase and installation of this capability into a designated section of our current facilities. The program will entail preparing the site, installation of the equipment, the hiring of skilled and non-skilled employees, training, and the startup of this operation. Our plan to accomplish this follows.

CHOICE OF SYSTEM

We have chosen Thisvi Systems Incorporated to furnish us with a customized system designed to meet our specifications. We believe that the ability to coat large parts will give us a competitive advantage in the marketplace we intend to serve.

Therefore, our system is designed to handle parts as large as 36" wide, 96" high, or 156" long.

Our system design will include a seven-stage spray washer:

Stage	Function
Stage 1	Pre-clean
State 2	Clean
Stave 3	Rinse
Stage 4	Condition rinse
Stage 5	Zinc phosphate
Stage 6	Rinse
Stage 7	Seal with D.I.
	Halo

This will be followed by a water dry-off oven dimensioned as 26' 2" high, 18' wide, and 106' 6" long.

This will be followed with a sealed coating room 39' 6" long, 71' wide, and 18' high. The room will be temperature controlled to 75 degrees with humidity of 50 ± 10%. The room will have a positive pressure.

A Nordson two-booth system will be contained in the room with the following characteristics:

- Able to paint parts 36" X 96" X 156"
- Two-booth system
- Automatic powder gun equipment
- Roll-off booths
- Reclaim system
- Booth control center with fire control
- Refrigerated air dry system

The complete system will have an overhead conveyor system 1,420' long with trolleys at 24" center, a maximum hook weight of 200 lbs, and a conveyor speed of 10' per minute. The production rated will be 15,000 pieces per hour.

This system will also have a transfer tunnel, a heat dissipation tunnel, and water blow off. Supporting the main system will be:

- Paint laboratory
- D.I. water unit

- Hook burn-off furnace
- Air make-up
- Waste treatment

SITE PREPARATION

The current site of the stamping tool room will be modified to accept the new powder coat system. All of the current flooring will be removed and replaced by an epoxy sealed floor. The structure of the tool room will be removed, including the current electrical layout. Selected obstructions will be removed as well as any remaining equipment. The walls will be coated appropriate to the new system, and new lighting will be installed in the whole area. The outside shipping docks will be modified to accept the appropriate amount of shipping. Supply conveyors will be installed as appropriate. This whole area will be sealed off from the contiguous areas of this facility to assure full compliance to required cleanliness. The roofing over this area will be repaired as necessary, and the necessary transformers will be installed to support the system.

The cost of this renovation is estimated at $500,000 and should take an estimated 18 weeks from the start of the project.

EQUIPMENT INSTALLATION

After approval of the project and signing of contracts, the timing for the installation of the system is set as follows.

- Complete drawings   Week 5
- Shipment of equipment to site   Week 18
- System operational   Week 25

HIRING AND TRAINING

The operation of this system requires skills not necessary for the current E-coat system. The primary future areas for hiring and training are in coating technology, operation of the system, and operation of the laboratory. In addition, the management of this operation will also require special training.

We plan to train our current management in the running of the operation and to hire the additional skills necessary. This will include an experienced system operator and laboratory technicians. Painters, hangers, and packers will be hired and trained by DEC personnel. The projected schedule for this is:

| Hiring of skilled personnel | 16 weeks prior to start-up |
| Hiring and training of labor | 3 weeks prior to start-up. |

In addition, departments such as Quality Assurance, Production Control, and Transportation will be expanded as appropriate to support this new business. Training is projected to cost $50,000.

PLANT START-UP

Pre-production start-up is expected to begin in Week 26 and continue for 4 weeks. Normal production in expected to commence in week 31.

PROJECT COSTS

Current estimates of project costs are as follows.

Site preparation	$500,000
System, including seven stage washer, holding tank, dry-off oven, bake oven, conveyor system, transfer tunnel, heat dissipation tunnel	$958,655
Nordson (2) booth system	$464,010
Reclaim powder equipment	42,090
D.I. water unit	33,850
Coating room	146,280
Hook burn-off furnace	26,485
Air makeup	35,220
Waste treatment	140,000
Surcharge for installation of Nordson equipment	55,681
Paint laboratory	50,000
	TOTAL $2,452,271

QUALITY ASSURANCE

Quality is the bedrock upon which our company will continue to grow and prosper. DEC's operating philosophy is to meet or exceed our customers' requirements on every part that we produce. We plan to be the "benchmark" against which our competitors measure their own performance.

To support the company's requirements, we plan to meet or exceed the following objectives.

1. Continue to involve all employees in the process of meeting or exceeding the customers' requirements.

2. Provide all employees with the necessary training to make a meaningful contribution to our quality standards and overall performance.

3. Develop and implement the systems and processes necessary to obtain QS-9000/ISO 9002 certification in early 1998, and ISO 14000 certification by the end of 1999.

4. Control all incoming material throughout the time it is in our process.

5. Develop systems to capture and make available to management the cost of non-conformance.

6. Vigorously pursue continual improvement.

EMPLOYEE INVOLVEMENT

Quality itself cannot be inspected. Only the person actually doing the work can meet our customers' requirements by doing it right the first, and every, time. This requires that we involve every employee in the quality process and provide them with the motivation, training, and tools to do the job right. At DEC, we have made that commitment. All employees have received substantial training in the tools of quality and in the skills necessary to use the tools of quality. Manufacturing management meets daily with workers to discuss the proper process and the level of quality necessary to meet or exceed customers' expectations. Any employee can refuse to hang a non-conforming part or at his/her option, and, if the process is not corrected to the appropriate and applicable procedures and/or standards, to shut down the line. An integral part of this involvement is our commitment to empowerment for all our employees and as such, all our systems are designed to support that process and we work at it every day. This is also one of the major areas of continual improvement.

QS-9000 CERTIFICATION

DEC fully recognizes that all future business with the OEM automotive companies and their suppliers will depend upon compliance with the new Quality System Requirements QS-9000. Other non-automotive companies will also soon require the same or similar level of compliance.

We are currently Q1 certified with Ford, "Green Light" Certified with General Motors, and self-certified to several Tier 1 customers. Our current focus is successful certification in QS-9000 by early 1998 and, continuing the path to improvement, certification in ISO 14000 by the end of 1999.

Utilizing a State of Michigan Training Grant, as well as our own resources, we are working with an experienced consultant to develop the systems necessary to obtain certification. Our Quality Manager is very experienced in the process and has experience obtaining certification for others. All employees have received substantial training in the systems and will continue to receive additional training as the process progresses. Managers who will be responsible for the accuracy and smooth working of various parts of the system are continuing to be trained in the systems and are providing necessary input to develop everything required.

LOT CONTROL

We are in the process of developing and implementing a lot control system for all incoming material. This system is the basis for tracking all material from receipt through shipment and will allow us to provide information on the progress of customer's parts at any stage of the process. It will also provide us with a record of the time the specific material was processed and when it was shipped. It will also tie in more directly to quality assurance and highlight any deviations from standard.

COST OF QUALITY

We are in the process of developing and implementing systems to track both the cost of quality and the cost of non-conformance. Quality costs will be broken out and reported separately. Information on the cost of non-conformance will be gathered, analyzed, and reported on a bi-weekly basis to all employees.

PROBLEM-SOLVING

A problem-solving team is in place and working in our coatings operation. The charter of the team is to identify problems, find root causes to these problems, and recommend solutions to management. We will expand this approach to both our stamping operation and to the office area. We have provided training to many employees in the tools of problem-solving and will expand this to others in the future.

HUMAN RELATIONS

DEC's employees are its most valuable asset. We provide a safe, clean environment that allows our employees to perform their jobs to the best of their abilities. To allow our employees to be of maximum benefit to the company in meeting its goals, Human Relations will pursue the following objectives.

1. Continue to improve communication throughout the company.
2. Provide functional cross-training to improve employees' skills and company flexibility.
3. Expeditiously handle any employee problems that are company-related to ensure a reliable work force.
4. Continue to administer the labor contract to ensure smooth relations with the U.A.W.

5. Take the lead in health and safety issues for our
   company.

EMPLOYEE RELATIONS

The Human Resources Department strives to ensure that all
our employees are able to work in an environment that will
enhance their productivity. We offer a full array of benefits
including company-paid medical and dental coverage, paid
vacations, and a 401K savings plan. Each new employee is
given a full orientation on DEC—benefits, workplace safety,
work rules, specific job requirements, and any other pertinent
information. We follow up with an evaluation of the employee
within 90 days of hire and monitor general performance over
time. We also supply—free of charge to the employee—any
required safety items such as safety glasses or ear plugs.

COMMUNICATION

Human Relations takes the lead in communicating with all
employees on items regarding the company, changes in work
rules, and safety and health issues. We also administer many
forms of employee training, assist other departments with
their training, and participate on cross-functional teams.

All pertinent news regarding quality, benefits updates, supplier and customer relations, new introduction of technology,
and the like is reported in the in-house newsletter, which is
published once a month and is distributed free of charge to
employees, suppliers, and customers.

BENEFITS ADMINISTRATION

We provide a very competitive level of benefits to enhance the
attractiveness of DEC to potential employees. Human Relations
administers all benefits plans—medical, dental, vacations, and
401K. While the medical and dental programs are administered
by the provider, we assist any employee that has questions
and/or concerns. All of the other programs require some level
of company management. We also handle all workers' compensation cases and unemployment insurance claims.

HEALTH AND SAFETY

We take substantial care to protect our employees. All workers in our plants are required to wear safety glasses, which we supply without charge. This includes employees who require prescription lenses. We also have available ear protection devices, and supply gloves to all employees everyday to protect both their hands and the customers' product. Safety meetings are held with all employees bi-weekly, and manufacturing management attends to individual safety items at daily meetings as appropriate. OSHA self-audits are conducted semi-annually to assure we are in compliance with all rules.

CONTRACT ADMINISTRATION

DEC has inherited the labor contract with Local 974 of the United Auto Workers from its prior company ABC Automotive Manufacturing Corporation. This contract runs through April 21, 1999. Our relations with the union are excellent. They are cooperative and helpful in most areas.

Human Relations administers all items relating to the contract, including grievances, seniority layoff, and hiring transfers between classifications and payroll. We administer all disciplinary matters and deal with our outside experts as necessary.

FINANCIAL

As with any successful company, DEC L.L.C. projects its financial results as a consequence of the actions anticipated in its business plan. To help in achieving these results, we plan to accomplish the following financial objectives.

1. Improve our cost tracking and control systems

2. Closely monitor our results against the business plan.

The results of our assumptions in this business plan are delineated in the financial schedules that accompany the plan, as part of the appendices. We expect that the achievement of the results anticipated in this plan will be a team effort and will be successful.

We continue to work at fine-tuning our cost tracking and control systems. As we progress, we anticipate our projections to be more in line with the real events and circumstances. This will allow us to take prompt action on necessary items, thereby reducing costs and improving performance.

We are firmly committed to investing in the growth of our business. We have identified the powder coat business as offering us the greatest potential for profitable growth. We are budgeting the necessary funds to enter this business and plan to secure these funds from a lender in the near future. Our financial projections reflect the securing of funds, their expenditure, and the expected results. As other opportunities present themselves and we are able to digest this expansion, we plan to pursue additional opportunities.

As a result of planned actions, we expect 1997 sales to be in the $8 million range. Future year plans reflect substantial growth in both our current business and the target new business segment reaching $20.5 million by 2001.

Income from operations for 1997 is expected to be $347,000. This is expected to improve substantially over the plan period to $2.8 million by 2001. Current year financials, through September 30, 1997, are included in this section.

Financial projections for the years 1998 to 2001 are also included in Appendix C. Included also are capital expenditures for the 1997–2001 period.

ASSUMPTIONS TO THE FINANCIAL PROJECTIONS

REVENUES

Revenues for the Electro-coating are estimated to grow by 19% in 1998 and in the range of 5 to 7% per year in 1999 to 2001. These projections are based on an analysis of current customers' ability to provide new business and on targeted new customers. During 1998, 60% of the additional revenue is expected to come from current customers and 40% from new customers. In the 1999 to 2001 period, 80% of the new revenue is expected to come from new customers.

Stamping revenue for 1998 reflects a full year as part of DEC and is projected to come from current customers. The growth in revenue in 1999 is expected to come from new customers that do business with our E-coat and powder coat operations. In 2000 and 2001, revenues are expected to reach maturity growth and therefore be level.

Powder coat revenues anticipate our beginning production in the third quarter of 1998 and increasing up to one full shift of production by the end of the year. Revenues from 1999 through 2001 reflect the addition of a second powder booth and new business from targeted customers to reach a capacity three-shift operation by 2001.

COST OF GOODS SOLD

Material costs are projected based upon current material costs for both the E-coat system, stamping, and the proposed powder coat system. These current costs take into account the purchase of certain customers' product, as this is expected to continue. Material cost for powder coating is expected to exceed current E-coat cost, so that 1998 projected costs of 20% of sales are expected to increase to 22% by 2001, reflecting the increase in powder coating as a percentage of total business.

Direct labor costs reflect the labor rates in effect with our labor contract and some assumptions regarding the continuation of that contract based on similar growth patterns. Direct labor hours have been estimated based upon job costing estimates. The new powder coating operation is not as labor-intensive as the existing E-coat operation, and therefore a lower labor cost of 14% has been projected.

Manufacturing burden consists of all other expenses related to the manufacturing operation of the company. Most of these expenses have been estimated based upon prior years' experience of the E-coat and stamping operations. Payroll taxes, employee insurance, and workers' compensation are based upon projected direct and indirect labor costs.

Rent is based upon the lease for the E-coat building and equipment and part of the stamping building and equipment between DEC, a related company, and a family trust. DEC will also lease the building where the new powder coat system is to be located, and rental rates will increase accordingly. Utilities, property insurance, and repairs and maintenance are estimates based upon prior experience in the industry.

SELLING, GENERAL, AND ADMINISTRATIVE (SG&A) EXPENSES

DEC is fully responsible for all SG&A expenses currently expended for all operations of the company. It is projected that these expenses will increase significantly as our new powder coat operation comes on line and then slowly fall as a percentage of total revenue as the operation reaches maturity.

INTEREST EXPENSE

Interest expense has been calculated at a rate of 10% on borrowings of $2.6 million. The amount represents the cost of the purchase, preparation, and installation of the powder coat system and its ancillary parts as well as ordinary capital expenditures for other parts of the business. The loan is expected to take place sometime during the 1998 and 1999 time frame.

CORPORATE TAXES

As no special tax situations are anticipated, this plan does not address corporate income taxes. If the need arises, this subject will also be addressed in depth.

Glossary

ACCELERATED LIFE TESTING—Verification of the machine and equipment design relationship much sooner than usual. Intended especially for new technology, design changes, and ongoing development.

ADVANCED STATISTICAL METHODS—More sophisticated and less widely applicable techniques of statistical process analysis and control than included in basic statistical methods. This can include more advanced control chart techniques, regression analysis, design of experiments, and advanced problem-solving techniques.

ANALYSIS OF VARIANCE (ANOVA) —Statistical method to evaluate the data from a designed experiment.

APPEARANCE ITEMS—Parts designated on engineering drawings as requiring approval for appearance characteristics including color, grain, texture, etc.

APQP—Advanced Product Quality Planning. See AQP.

AQM—Advanced Quality Management - Overall quality management, starting at the design of the product/process and continuing through the manufacture and shipment of the product to the customer.

AQP—Advanced Quality Planning. See APQP and AQM. AQP is a structured method for defining and executing the actions necessary to ensure a product that satisfies the customer. AQP is an integrated, structured team approach required of all system, subsystem, and component design, process, and service. It is optimized through:

—open communication

—team synergy

—team consensus

ATTRIBUTE DATA—Qualitative data that can be counted for recording and analysis. Examples include characteristics such as the presence of a required label, the installation of all required fasteners, and the absence of errors on an expense report.

AVERAGE—The sum of values divided by the number (sample size) of values; designated by a bar over the symbol for the values being averaged: e.g., X (X bar) is the average of the X values within a subgroup; X (X double bar) is the average of subgroup averages; X (X tilde-bar) is the average of subgroup medians; p (p bar) is the average of p's from all the subgroups. (See also means.)

AWARENESS—Personal understanding of the interrelationship of quality and productivity by directing attention to the requirement for management commitment and statistical thinking to achieve never-ending improvement.

BASIC STATISTICAL METHODS— Applies the theory of variation through use of basic problem-solving techniques and statistical process control: includes control chart construction and interpretation (for both variables and attribute data) and capability analysis.

BINOMIAL DISTRIBUTION— A discrete probability distribution for attribute data that applies to conforming and nonconforming units and underlies the p and np charts.

BLACK BOX (PROPRIETARY ASSEMBLY) —An assembly purchased by the customer, the components of which are designed by the supplier, and for which a performance specification only has been developed by the customer.

BLACK BOX TESTING—Testing for acceptability of external output given specified external inputs and without concern for intermediate internal functions.

BROWN BOX TESTING—Testing for acceptability of external output given specified external inputs and with some specific concerns for intermediate internal functions.

CAPABILITY—(Can be determined only after the process is in statistical control) When the process average plus and minus the 3σ spread of the distribution of individuals (X + or -3σ) is contained within the specification tolerance (variables data), or when at least 99.73% of data points are within specification (attributes data), a process is said to be capable. Effort to improve capability must, however, be consistent with the operational philosophy of never-ending improvement in quality and productivity.

CAUSE AND EFFECT DIAGRAM—A simple tool for individual or group problem-solving that shows the various process elements to analyze potential sources of process variation. Also called fishbone diagram (after its appearance) or Ishikawa diagram (after its developer).

CENTRAL LINE—The line on a control chart that represents the average or median value of the items being plotted.

CHARACTERISTICS— Distinguishing features of a process or its output based on the idea that variables or attributes data can be collected.

COMMON CAUSE—A source of variation that affects all the individual values of the process output being studied; in control chart analysis it appears as part of the random process variation.

CONSECUTIVE—Units of output produced in succession; a basis for selecting subgroup samples.

CONTROL CHART—A graphic representation of a characteristic of a process, showing plotted values of the same statistic gathered from a central line and one or two control limits. It minimizes the net economic loss from Type 1 and Type 2 errors. It has two basic uses: as a judgment to determine if a process has been operating in statistical control, and as an operation to aid in maintaining statistical control.

CONTROL ITEMS—Products (parts, assemblies, materials) identified on drawings and specifications with a symbol preceding the part/specification number(s) and which contain one or more critical characteristics.

CONTROL LIMITS—Lines on control charts that define the limits of the natural variation of a process. Variation beyond a control limit is evidence that special causes are affecting the process. Control limits relate to statistics calculated from process data and must not be confused with engineering specifications.

CONTROL PLANS—Documents describing the system for controlling production processes. Producers must establish control plans for all new products and must address all significant and critical design characteristics, process parameters, and engineering standard tests.

COVARIANCE—Measure of how two variables change together.

CQIS—Common quality indicator system. A mainframe computer software system that is designed to store and report data for early detection or emerging problems.

C_p - (process potential) —An index that is the ratio of the tolerance range to the six sigma process spread without regard to location of the data. It must be calculated only

after establishing that the process is in statistical control.

C_{pk} - (process capability per thousand) —An index that considers both the process spread and the proximity of the process spread to specification limits. It must be calculated only after establishing that the process is in statistical control.

CRITICAL CHARACTERISTICS— Product requirements (dimensions, specifications, tests) or process parameters that can affect compliance with government regulations or safety product functions and also require specific producer, assembly, shipping, or monitoring actions and inclusion on control plans. Critical characteristics are identified with signs and noted on customer drawings and specifications. Typical signs are the diamond and inverted delta.

DERATING—The practice of limiting stresses which may be applied to a component to levels below the specified maxima, in order to enhance reliability. Derating values of electrical stress are expressed as ratios of applied stress to rated maximum stress. The applied stress is taken as the maximum likely to be applied during worst case operating conditions. Thermal aerating is expressed as a temperature value.

DESIGN OF EXPERIMENTS (DOE) —A plan to conduct tests that involves all of the prework that must be accomplished before any tests are conducted. Prework requirements are: questions are written; data collection sheets are prepared; analysis of data is laid out; and the limitations of the test are known. DOE focuses on identifying factors that affect the level or magnitude of a product/process response examining the response surface and forming the mathematical prediction model.

DESIGN REVIEWS—A review providing in-depth detail relative to the evolving design supported by drawings, process flow descriptions,. engineering analyses, reliability design features, and maintainability design considerations.

DETECTION—A past-oriented strategy that attempts to identify unacceptable output after it has been produced and then to separate it from the good output.

DEVIATION—A reporting document for revealing product concerns with customer operations. The deviation serves as an engineering part/process modification form. The form is used to notify the system that changes have occurred.

DRY RUN—The rehearsal or cycling of machinery, normally with the intent of not processing the work piece, to verify: function, clearances, and construction stability.

DURABILITY—Ability to perform intended function over a specified period under normal use with specified maintenance, without significant deterioration.

EIGHT-DISCIPLINE (8-D) APPROACH—An orderly, team-oriented approach to problem-solving. Also referred to as a concern analysis report or TOPS (team oriented problem-solving)

ENGINEERING MATERIAL SPECIFICATIONS—Documents that describe a product's material and define its technical requirements that control function, endurance, performance, and physical and mechanical properties. They also contain approved test methods for evaluating conformance with such requirements for that material.

ENGINEERING SPECIFICATIONS—Documents that contain information that is necessary to produce or evaluate parts and components. Specifications are usually issued with engineering drawings. Information is contained in the specification that relates to function, performance, and durability tests.

EQUIPMENT—The portion of process machinery which is not specific to a component or sub-assembly.

FAILURE—An event when machinery/equipment is not available to produce parts under specified conditions when scheduled, or is not capable of producing parts or performing scheduled operations to specifications. For every failure, an action is required.

FAILURE MODE AND EFFECTS ANALYSIS (FMEA)—Technique to identify each potential failure mode and its effect on machinery performance, processes, or product design.

FAILURE REPORTING, ANALYSIS, AND CORRECTIVE ACTION SYSTEM (FRACAS) — An orderly system of recording and transmitting failure data from the supplier's plant to the end users resides in a unitary database. The database allows identification of pattern failures and rapid resolution of problems through rigorous failure analysis. It includes at least five distinct and basic sequential and interactive functions. They are:

1. Recording data about individual failure incidents at first, often manually later, often automatically on a formal failure report or data structure.
2. Reporting data to an analysis group of engineers members who are responsible to do something about each failure.
3. Analysis of individual failures or series of related failures to discover the causes of failures to recommend or initiate corrective action.
4. Forwarding engineering oriented correction plans once the cause of failure is known to functional groups responsible for taking corrective action.
5. Checking on corrective action adequacy to see if further action is required to close the loop on the initial failures; revise and repeat corrective action if necessary.

FAME (forecasted and available machinery and equipment)— Web-based tool used during the machinery and equipment disposition process to advertise reusable surplus machinery and equipment. To allow other operations to consider reuse, machinery and equipment information should be entered into FAME as soon as it is known that the equipment will be displaced.

FAULT TREE ANALYSIS (FTA) — A top-down approach to failure analysis starting with an undesirable event and determining all the ways it can happen.

FEASIBILITY—A determination that a process, design, procedure, or plan can be successfully accomplished in the required time frame.

FINITE ELEMENT ANALYSIS (FEA) —A computational structural analysis technique that quantifies a structure's response to applied loading conditions. It may be used as a modeling tool in the early design and development phase of a product.

GAGE ACCURACY—Difference between the observed average of measurement and the master average of the same parts using precision instruments.

GAGE LINEARITY—Difference in the accuracy values of a gage through the expected operating range of the gage.

GAGE REPEATABILITY—Variation in measurements obtained with one gage when used several times by one operator while measuring a characteristic on one part.

GAGE REPRODUCIBILITY— Variation in the average of the measurement made by different operators using the same gage when measuring a characteristic on one part.

GAGE STABILITY—Total variation in the measurements obtained with a gage on the same master or master parts when measuring a characteristic over an extended time period.

GAGE SYSTEM ERROR—The combination of gage accuracy, repeatability, reproducibility, stability, and linearity.

GRAY BOX—An assembly purchased by the customer, for which the producer has design, development, and detail drawing responsibility, but for which the customer provides design or material specification inputs.

HISTOGRAM—A pictorial way to display data in showing frequency of occurrence.

IMPLEMENTATION TESTING—Testing of a procedure, product, or feature during its development that is performed by the designer who is implementing it. A form of "white testing." The implementation tests generated during this period should allow maximum exposure at minimal cost, operator execution, and self checking.

IN CONTROL—State of a process when it exhibits only random variation (as opposed to systematic variations and/or variations with assignable sources).

INDICES—Used to compare the variation and/or central tendency of a product characteristic or process parameter to specification.

INITIAL SAMPLES—Small quantities of products taken from a significant production run made with production tooling, processes, and cycle times. Initial samples are checked by the producer for conformance to every product requirement on the applicable drawings and/or specifications.

IN-PROCESS TEST—Durability or function tests required by engineering to monitor a specific

design requirement on a continuous basis during production. Reaction plans and sampling frequencies for these tests must be included in the control plan.

INSPECTION—Activities such as measuring, examining, testing, or gagging one or more characteristics of a product or service and comparing these with specified requirements.

INTERACTION—Found in gage R&R . Known activity between operator and part. Operator differences depend on the part being measured.

LIFE CYCLE—The sequence through which machinery and equipment pass from conception through decommission.

LIFE CYCLE COSTS (LCC)—The sum of all cost factors incurred during the expected life of the machinery.

LONG-TERM CAPABILITY—Statistical measure within subgroup variation exhibited by a process over a long period of time. Typically it includes the entire natured cycle of the process. This differs from performance because it does not include the between subgroup variation.

LOT—A quantity of a product produced under similar conditions so that the product within the lot is expected to be homogeneous in all significant attributes .

LOWER CONTROL LIMIT (LCL)—For control charts: the limit which the process must remain to be in control.

MACHINE CONDITION SIGNATURE ANALYSIS (MCSA)—Reliability, maintainability, and durability: an application that applies mechanical signature (vibration) analysis techniques to characterize machinery and equipment on a systems level to significantly improve reliability and maintainability.

MACHINERY—Tooling and equipment combined. A generic term for all hardware (including necessary operational software) which performs in a manufacturing process.

MAINTAINABILITY—A characteristic of design, installation, and operation, usually expressed as the probability that a machine can be retained in, or restored to, a specified operable condition within a specified interval of time when maintenance is performed in accordance with prescribed procedures.

MEAN—The average of values in a group of measurements.

MEAN TIME BETWEEN FAILURES (MTBF) —The average time between failure occurrences. The sum of the operating time of a machine divided by the total number of failures. Predominantly used for repairable equipment.

MEAN TIME TO FAILURE (MTTF) —The average time to failure for a specific equipment design. Used predominantly for non-repairable equipment.

MEAN TIME TO REPAIR (MTTR) —The average time to restore machinery or equipment to specified conditions.

NEVER ENDING IMPROVEMENT IN QUALITY AND PRODUCTIVITY— The operational philosophy that makes best use of the talent within the company to produce products of increasing quality for customers in an increasingly efficient way that protects the return on investment to the stockholders. This is a dynamic strategy designed to enhance the strength of the company in the face of present and future market conditions. It contrasts with any static strategy that accepts some particular level of outgoing defects as inevitable.

NON-CONFORMING UNITS— Units which do not conform to a specification or other inspection standard; sometimes called discrepant or defective units. The p and np control charts are used to analyze systems producing nonconforming units.

NON-CONFORMITIES—Specific occurrences of a condition which does not conform to specification or other inspection standards; sometimes called discrepancies or defects. An individual nonconforming unit can have the potential for more than one nonconformity (e.g., a door could have several dents and dings; a functional check of a carburetor could reveal any of a number of potential discrepancies). c, p, and u control charts are used to analyze systems producing nonconformities.

NORMAL DISTRIBUTION— A continuous, symmetrical, bell-shaped frequency distribution for variables data that underlies the control charts for variables. When measurements have a normal distribution, about 68.26% of all data points lie within plus or minus one standard deviation limits of the mean, about 95.44% of all data points lie within plus or minus two standard deviation limits of the mean, and about 99.73% lie within plus or minus three standard deviation limits of the mean. These percentages are the basis for control limits and control chart analysis and for many capability decisions.

OUT-OF-CONTROL—Condition describing a process from which all special causes of variation have not been eliminated. This condition is evident on a control chart by the presence of points outside the control limits or by patterns that are not random within the control limits.

OVERALL EQUIPMENT EFFECTIVENESS (OEE) — Percentage of the time the machinery is available (Availability) x how fast the machinery is running relative to its design cycle (Performance efficiency) x percentage of the resulting product within quality specifications (Yield).

PARETO CHART—A tool for problem-solving that involves ranking potential problem areas or sources of variation, according to their contribution to cost or to total variation. Typically, a few causes account for most of the cost (or variation), so problem-solving efforts are best prioritized to concentrate on the "vital few" causes, temporarily ignoring the "trivial many." The graph depicts the causes in a descending order of importance.

PARSER (Product analysis, reliability, and service evaluation report)—Provides details and customer defined aggregate reporting in the form of segmented, specified data for the purpose of analysis.

PERISHABLE TOOLING—Tooling which is consumed over time, during a manufacturing operation.

PLANT FLOOR INFORMATION SYSTEM (PFIS) —An information gathering system used on the plant floor to gather data relating to plant operations including maintenance activities.

P_p: Preliminary process potential similar to C_p—process potential— It is used in the early stages of prototyping and when data is limited. However, stability must be established before this index is used.

P_{pk}: Preliminary process capability similar to C_{pk} - process capability— It is used in the early stages of prototyping and when data are limited. However, stability must be established before this index is used.

PPM—Parts per million.

PREDICTIVE MAINTENANCE (PdM)— A portion of scheduled maintenance dedicated to inspection for the purpose of detecting incipient failures.

PREVENTATIVE MAINTENANCE (PM) —Reliability, maintainability, and durability: a portion of scheduled maintenance dedicated to taking planned actions for the purpose of reducing the frequency or severity of future failures, including lubrication, filter changes, and part replacement dictated by analytical techniques and predictive maintenance procedures.

PREVENTION—A future-oriented strategy that improves quality and productivity by directing analysis and action toward correcting the process itself. Prevention is consistent with a philosophy of never-ending improvement.

PROBABILITY RATIO SEQUENTIAL TESTING (PRST) — A reliability qualification test to demonstrate if the machinery/equipment satisfies a specified MTBF requirement and is not lower than an acceptable MTBF. (MIL-STD-781)

PROCESS—Any operation or sequence of operations which contributes to the transformation of raw material into a finished part or assembly. It is a singular factor or a combination of factors made up of: people, equipment, machine, method, measurement, environment, and materials that produce a product or service.

PROCESS CAPABILITY—The ability of the process to be consistent and predictable. The variation of the process is within the specifications as well as the upper and lower control limits. As a consequence, the only variation of a capable process is the common one. This variation will always be present in the process, and the capability measured is the best the process will ever produce unless changed.

PROCESS CONTROL—Means to control the output of a process by gathering data about it. May include the use of controls such as SPC techniques and the establishment of a feedback loop to prevent the manufacture of nonconforming products.

PROCESS FAILURE MODE AND EFFECTS ANALYSIS (FMEA) —An analytical technique which identifies the potential failure modes of a process and their causes to prioritize

improvement opportunities. The FMEA should be treated as a living document that is updated as necessary whenever process changes.

PROCESS PERFORMANCE— Statistical measure of all types of variation exhibited by a process, including within subgroup and between subgroups. Performance is determined from a process study which is conducted over an extended period of time under normal operating conditions.

PROCESS VARIATION —Common cause and special cause variation of a process; process capability.

PRODUCTION—In relation to tooling and equipment suppliers, refers to the "process" required to produce the product.

QUALITY—Total features or characteristics of a product or service that determine its ability to satisfy customer needs.

QUALITY CONTROL—The operations, techniques, and activities used to fulfill the requirements of quality.

R/1000—Repair per thousand.

RANGE—Difference between the smallest and the largest values in a set of observations.

R & M PLAN—Establishes a clear implementation strategy for design assurance techniques, reliability testing and assessment, and R & M continuous improvement activities during the machinery/equipment life cycle.

R & M TARGETS—The range of values that MTBF and MTTR are expected to fall between, plus an improvement factor which leads to MTBF and MTTR requirements.

RAPID—A process improvement approach which identifies and removes wasteful and unnecessary work in business processes. Focuses on improvement actions which are easily implemented and have relatively high pay-off to the business.

RELIABILITY—The probability that machinery and equipment can perform continuously, without failure, for a specified interval of time when operating under stated conditions.

RELIABILITY.GROWTH—Machine reliability improvement as a result of identifying and eliminating machinery or equipment failure caused during machine testing and operations.

ROOT CAUSE ANALYSIS (RCA) — A logical, systematic approach to identifying the basic reasons (causes, mechanisms, etc.) for a problem, failure, non-conformance, process error, etc. The result of root cause analysis should always be the identification of the source of the problem and a recommendation for corrective action.

SAMPLE—One or more individual events or measurements selected from the output of a process.

SCATTER DIAGRAM—A plot of two variables, one against the other, to display trends.

SE-II—A special warranty system that Ford Motor Company uses. It consists of two parts: a) customer run, which is an online warranty information tool offering management and problem solvers at all levels the opportunity to analyze warranty repair information; and b) time-based quality indicators,

which are an application system used to report and analyze warranty repair and things gone wrong with data over time.

SEVEN PLANNING and MANAGEMENT TOOLS—Also known as the "new tools" of quality. They are: affinity diagram, relations diagram or interrelationship diagram, tree diagram, prioritization matrices, matrix diagram, process decision program chart, and activity network diagram.

SIGNIFICANT CHARACTERISTICS—Process, product, and test requirements which are important for customer satisfaction and for which quality planning actions must be summarized on a control plan.

SIMULTANEOUS ENGINEERING (SE) —Product engineering which optimizes the final product by the proper integration of requirements, including product function, manufacturing and assembly processing, service engineering, and disposal.

SPECIAL CAUSES—Intermittent source of variation that is unpredictable or unstable; sometimes called an assignable cause. Signaled by a point beyond the control limits or a run or other nonrandom pattern within the control limits.

SPECIFICATION—The engineering requirements for evaluating acceptability of a particular characteristic. A specification may or may not be consistent with the demonstrated capability of the process. A specification is not the same as a control limit.

STANDARD DEVIATION—Measure of spread of a set of values about their average value.

STATISTICAL CONTROL—Condition describing a process from which all special causes of variation have been eliminated and only common causes remain. Shown on a control chart by the absence of points outside the control limits and by the absence of nonrandom patterns or trends within the control limits.

STATISTICAL PROCESS CONTROL—The use of statistical methods such as X bar and R charts (as well as other types of control charts) to analyze a process's output. Charts are then used to determine appropriate actions to take to achieve and maintain statistical control and to improve the capability of the process.

SUBGROUP—For control chart files: group of items from a process, sampled at or near the same time.

SUPPLIER QUALITY ASSISTANCE (SQA) —The activity within the automotive industry that is responsible for contacts with suppliers regarding quality. SQA assists suppliers with developing systems for prevention of defects and continuing reduction of process variability.

SYSTEM—A number of parts that are interdependent and linked in a coherent way to each other. A system can also refer to a group of interrelated processes linked to produce products.

TESTING— A means of determining the capability of an item to meet specified requirements by subjecting the item to a set of physical, chemical, environmental, or operating actions and conditions.

THINGS GONE RIGHT VERSUS THINGS GONE WRONG (TGR/TGW) —An evolving program-level compilation of lessons learned that captures successful and unsuccessful manufacturing engineering activity and equipment and/or performance for feedback to the organization and its suppliers for continuous improvement.

TOOLING—The portion of the process machinery which is specific to a component of sub-assembly.

TOTAL PRODUCTIVE MAINTENANCE (fTPM) —Natural cross-functional groups working together in an optimal balance to improve the overall effectiveness of their equipment and processes within their work areas. TPM implementation vigorously benchmarks, measures, and corrects all losses resulting from inefficiencies.

UPPER CONTROL LIMIT (UCL) —For control charts: the limit below which a process must remain to be in control.

VARIABLES DATA—Measurements taken on a continuous scale.

VARIATION—Change in the value of a measured characteristic. Sources of variation can be grouped into two major classes: common causes and special causes.

WHITE BOX TESTING—Testing internal functions which must collectively result in the specified external output.

Bibliography

Allen, C. Wesley. *Simultaneous engineering.* Society of Manufacturing Engineering. Dearborn, MI.

American Society for Quality Control (1971). *Quality costs: What and how.* American Society for Quality Control. Milwaukee, WI.

American Society for Quality Control (1977). *Guide for reducing quality costs.* American Society for Quality Control. Milwaukee, WI.

American Society for Quality Control (January, 1980). *Guide for managing vendor quality costs.* American Society for Quality Control. Milwaukee, WI.

American Society for Quality Control (1986). *Product recall planning guide.* American Society for Quality Control. Milwaukee, WI.

American Society for Quality Control, Quality Costs Committee (1987). *Guide for reducing quality costs.* American Society for Quality Control. Milwaukee, WI.

ANSI/ASQC. Standard B1-1958 and B2-1958. *Guide for quality control and control chart method of analyzing data.* American Society for Quality Control. Milwaukee, WI.

ANSI/ASQC. Standard B3-1958. *Control chart method of controlling quality during production.* American Society for Quality Control. Milwaukee, WI.

Armstrong, D (!993-1994). "Planning and Organizing for Quality in a Human Resources Department." Vol. 6. No. 2. *Quality Engineering.*

Broh, R.A. (1982). *Managing quality for higher profits.* McGraw-Hill Book Company. NY, NY.

Brown, M.G. (December 1991). "Developing a plan to win Malcolm Baldrige National Quality Award." *Journal for Quality and Participation.*

Burr, John T. (June 1990). "The Tools of Quality." *Quality Progress.*

Cassell, R.H. (October 1991). "Preproduction Quality Planning: What's It All About?" *Quality Digest.*

Chrysler, Ford and General Motors (1995). *Measurement and system analysis: Reference manual.* Chrysler, Ford, and General Motors. Distributed by Automotive Industry Action Group. Southfield, MI.

Chrysler, Ford and General Motors (1995). *Potential failure mode and effect analysis: Reference manual.* Chrysler, Ford, and General Motors. Distributed by Automotive Industry Action Group. Southfield, MI.

Chrysler, Ford, and General Motors (1995). *Advanced product quality planning and control plan: Reference manual.* Chrysler, Ford, and General Motors. Distributed by Automotive Industry Action Group. Southfield, MI.

Chrysler, Ford, and General Motors (1996). *Quality system requirements: QS-9000.* Chrysler, Ford, and General Motors. Distributed by Automotive Industry Action Group. Southfield, MI.

Chrysler, Ford, and General Motors (1995). *Statistical process control: Reference manual.* Chrysler, Ford, and General Motors. Distributed by Automotive Industry Action Group. Southfield, MI.

Chrysler, Ford, and General Motors (1995). *Production part approval process.* Chrysler, Ford, and General Motors. Distributed by Automotive Industry Action Group. Southfield, MI.

Chrysler Corporation (August 1988). *SQA Guide to System Requirements.* Supplier Quality/Procurement and Supply Office. Chrysler Corporation. Highland Park, MI.

Coleman, H.W. and Steele, W.G. (1989). *Experimentation and uncertainty analysis for engineers.* John Wiley and Sons. NY, NY.

DePriest, D.J. and Launer, R.L. (1983). *Reliability in the acquisitions process.* Vol. 4. Marcel Dekker. NY, NY.

Dodson, B. (1994). *Weibull analysis.* Quality Press. Milwaukee, WI.

Duncan, A.J. (1986). *Quality control and industrial statistics.* 5th ed. R.D. Irwin, Inc. Homewood, IL.

Feigenbaun, A.V. (1983). *Total quality control.* 3rd ed. McGraw-Hill Book Company. NY, NY.

Flynn, B.B. (Winter 1995). Determinants of Quality Performance in High- and Low-Quality Plants." *Quality Management Journal.*

Ford Motor Company (December 1990). *Machine capability studies.* Product Quality Office. Ford Motor Company. Dearborn, MI.

Ford Motor Company (1988). *Packaging and shipping guide.* Material Handling Engineer, Ford Motor Company. Dearborn, MI.

Ford Motor Company (March 1988). *Supplier quality improvement guidelines for prototypes.* NAAO Production Purchasing. Ford Motor Company. Dearborn, MI.

Ford Motor Company (January 1989). *Team oriented problem solving.* Ford Motor Company. Power Train Operations. Dearborn, MI.

Ford Planning for Quality (January 1990). *Total quality excellence and systems management.* 2nd printing. Corporate Quality Office. Ford Motor Company. Dearborn, MI.

Ford Planning for Quality (April 1990). *Initial sample review process.* Quality Office. Ford Motor Company. Dearborn, MI.

Freedman, W. (1984). *Products liability for corporate counsels, controllers, and product safety executives.* Van Nostrand Reinhold Company. NY, NY.

Gevirtz, C. (April 1991). "Fundamentals of Advanced Quality Planning." *Quality Progress.*

Green, A.E. (1983). *Safety systems reliability.* John Wiley and Sons. NY, NY.

Grim, A.F. (Ed.) (1984). *Quality costs: Ideas and applications.* American Society for Quality Control. Milwaukee, WI.

Hagan, J.T. (Ed.) (1986). *Principles of quality costs.* American Society for Quality Control. Milwaukee, WI.

Harrington, H.J. (1987). *Poor-quality cost.* Marcel Dekker. NY, NY.

Hercules, J. (1996). "Terminal Boxes with Insertion Strips: Advanced Planning of the Quality and Validation of the Design." Vol. 8, No. 4. *Quality Engineering.*

Huthwaite, Bart (October 1989). "The Link Between Design and Activity Based Accounting." *Manufacturing Systems.*

Ireson, W. Grant and Coombs Jr., C.F. (1988). *Handbook of reliability engineering and management.* McGraw Hill Book Company. NY, NY.

Jolivet, F. (January 1985). "Safety and QA in Nuclear Power

Plants: A Quality Management Standard." *Quality Progress.*

Juran, J.M. (1988). *Quality control handbook.* Fourth Edition. McGraw Hill. NY. NY.

Kaufman, R. (September/October 1996). "Visions Strategic Planning and Quality—More Than Hype." *Educational Technology.*

Kaufman, R. (May/June 1995). "Beyond Conventional Benchmarking: Integrating Ideal Visions, Strategic Planning, and Reengineering." *Educational Technology.*

Kaufman, R. and English, F.W. (1979). *Needs assessment: Concept and application.* Educational Technology Publications. Englewood, NJ.

Kluge, R.H. (December 1996). "An Incentive Compensation Plan With an Eye on Quality." *Quality Progress.*

Larson, M. (June 1997). "Bright Ideas Enhance Plan Floor Quality." *Quality.*

Lloyd, D.K. and Lipow, M. (1984). *Reliability: Management, methods, and mathematics.* American Society for Quality Control, Milwaukee, WI.

O'Connor, P.D.T. (1985). *Practical reliability engineering.* 2nd ed. John Wiley and Sons. NY, NY.

Petersen, Bob (February 1991). "Production Scheduling Optimizes the Edge." *Manufacturing Systems.*

Rice, E. (Ed.) (No Date). *A quick reference guide for team building.* Ford North American Automotive Operations. Dearborn, MI.

Rossett, A. (1987). *Training needs assessment.* Educational Technology Publications. Englewood, NJ.

Russell, J.P. (April 1991). "Six Point Quality Planning." *Quality Progress.*

Shertz, R.S. (January 1988). "Effecting a Quality Plan of Action." *Quality.*

Shingo, S. (1986). *Zero quality control: Source inspection and the Poka-yoke system.* Trans. A.P. Dillon. Productivity Press. Cambridge, MA.

Spurga, D.C. (1987). *Balance sheet basics.* A Mentor Book. New American Library. NY, NY.

Stamatis, D.H. (1998). *Implementing the TE supplement.* Quality Resources. NY. NY.

Stamatis, D.H. (1997). *Total quality management engineering handbook.* Marcel Dekker. NY, NY.

Stamatis, D.H. (1996). *Integrating QS-9000 with your automotive system.* 2nd ed. Quality Press. Milwaukee, WI.

Stamatis, D.H. (1996). *Documenting and auditing for ISO 9000 and QS-9000.* Irwin Professionals. Chicago, IL.

Stamatis, D.H. (1995). *Failure mode and effect analysis: FMEA from theory to execution.* Quality Press. Milwaukee, WI.

Swift, J.A. (1989). "Methodology for Developing a Quality Plan Within a Manufacturing Company." *Quality Engineering.* Vol. 1, No. 4.

Tsuda & Tribus (April 1991). Planning the Quality Visit." *Quality Progress.*

Winchell, W.O. (Ed.) (1987). *Guide for managing supplier quality costs.* 2nd ed. American Society for Quality Control. Milwaukee, WI.

Index

Printed in the United States
47732LVS00002B/1-75